Teach Us to Pray

STUDY GUIDE

THIRTEEN LESSONS FOR INDIVIDUAL OR GROUP STUDY

RAY PETTY

Melbourne, Florida USA

TEACH US TO PRAY STUDY GUIDE—Thirteen Lessons for Individual or Group Study
by Ray Petty

Parsons Publishing House
P. O. Box 410063
Melbourne, FL 32941 USA
www.ParsonsPublishingHouse.com
Info@ParsonsPublishingHouse.com

Publisher has opted to reference satan and related names with lowercase letters.

ISBN-13: 978-1602731080
ISBN-10: 160273108X
Printed in the United States of America.
For World-Wide Distribution.

What Are People Saying?

⌘

A good prayer life is one of the most important components of being a strong disciple. Ray has his own unique style. His fresh insights into the inner workings of prayer will help everyone. If you are looking for a good small group/individual resource, this book is an excellent way to build a powerful prayer life. Having been on the receiving end of Ray's prayers, I can testify that he knows how to pray with power. This book is an outgrowth of his passion for making disciples of Jesus Christ. —Rick Spell, Pastor, Glendale UMC, Morristown, TN.

I imagine every one of us has at one point or another questioned whether we are able to clearly hear the voice of God or whether our prayers are effective. For the mature Christian, Pastor Ray's study guide, ***Teach Us to Pray,*** will increase your faith. For those just starting out on their Christian faith journey, it's an invaluable tool when it comes to learning about effective communication with God which is the cornerstone of a relationship with Christ. As a campus pastor, I believe this teaching study guide to be an invaluable tool for training and discipleship. Although it was created with group study in mind, it is well suited for individual use as well. —Ryan McCrillis, Director of Student Ministries, Knox CHOP, University of Tennessee, Knoxville, TN.

For any who sincerely desire to increase their understanding of the why and how of prayer, and also wish to become more effective in prayer, I recommend the reading and study of this book by Ray Petty, Jr. It is solidly based on Holy Scripture, doctrinally correct and practical, and written in language easily understood. The questions with each chapter are excellent for self-examination and discovery and for interactive discussion. The subject of the book is dealt with thoroughly, but also concisely. Conveniently divided into 13 lessons, it is perfectly suited for a quarter of weekly lessons taught as an elective in Sunday school or for weekday Bible study groups. It is also equally well-suited for individual study. It strongly emphasizes the believer's identity with Christ, fellowship with God the Father, and the importance of Holy Spirit-filled living. —DANIEL L. BLACK, TH.D., EDITOR/WRITER, PATHWAY PRESS, CLEVELAND, TN.

In forty-seven years of full-time ministry, I have never been more spiritually enlightened, divinely encouraged, and scripturally instructed about the "call" to live a life of constant prayer. The "keys" of the kingdom of prayer that are given in this book will definitely "unlock" the flow of supernatural living in your daily life. —DR. JON L. JENKINS, EVANGELIST, IN HOUSE MINISTRY, TROUTMAN, NC.

For every follower of Jesus Christ, there is nothing more important than prayer. This is the one thing the first disciples asked of Jesus, and it is the most important thing for us to ask today. ***Teach Us To Pray*** is a book that is rooted in Scripture and rich with insight from a passionate pastor with proven effectiveness in ministry. You will enjoy the content of the lessons and the insights that emerge from the questions at the end of each chapter. This is a great resource for individual and small groups. —REV. TOM ALBIN, DIRECTOR OF SPIRITUAL FORMATION AND CONGREGATIONAL LIFE, THE UPPER ROOM, NASHVILLE, TN.

Acknowledgments

⌘

I want to express my sincere gratitude and thanks to my wife, Alice, who spent hours reading and rereading this work. It is through her help and commitment that I can get into the hands of others this practical study on prayer. We trust that others will be blessed through this work and will be encouraged to grow in their prayer life by becoming persons of prayer.

This study on prayer began as a class offered to a lay speaker training class that I was leading. After teaching this course, the Lord said, "I want you to take this further and develop it as a teaching and training tool to equip others to pray powerfully and boldly." So the Lord had me add six additional lessons to teach on the different aspects of prayer. I believe this teaching tool can take us to new levels in prayer and new ways of praying as we build intimacy with the Lord into our lives. Intimacy with Jesus Christ, Father God, and the Holy Spirit is the key that unlocks doors that have been previously closed and opens doors that we thought would be impossible. So get ready for the new thing God is about to impart to you.

Table of Contents

⌘

Introduction

Following my encounter with Jesus Christ, I had a desire to pray and to seek the heart of God. My pastor and his wife would put books on prayer into my hands when I was a teenager, and my love for fellowship and intimacy with the Father grew as a result of that. Prayer has been the seedbed of learning to walk with Jesus and learning to hear His voice. Prayer is the place where faith is released, declared, and decreed that the purpose, plan, and will of God be known. Through this book, my hope and prayer for you is that it creates a strong desire to go deeper and to go higher in your prayer life—to experience a deep fellowship and intimacy with the Father resulting in your greatest hope being for His presence and nothing else will do. Prayer is expressing our love for the One who loves us the most and inviting the Lover of our soul into every area of our lives.

You have picked up this material because you desire to grow in your prayer life, to become more bold and courageous in prayer, and to encounter the presence of God amid your prayer. You want to move from being a person who prays to become a praying person. You have been looking to tap into the river of God's Spirit so what flows through you is the life of the Son of God.

Today may be the starting point, the launching pad, for you to begin moving into the area of prayer that G. Campbell Morgan describes:

> "See what I can do without the things you are depending on. See what I can do in answer to a praying people. See what I can do through the simplest who are ready to depend wholly and absolutely upon Me" (***The Welsh Revival***, London, 1905).

These are the days when God is looking to and fro for those who will stand in the gap and pray until something happens. I believe God is looking for a praying people who intercede—to be change agents through powerful prayer. Prayer is making ourselves available to Him and allowing Him to use us in whatever He desires. Prayer is learning to co-labor with Christ in bringing His Kingdom to be a present reality where we are.

> The first thing in prayer is to get God. If you get Him, everything else follows...allow God to get at you, to invade you, to take possession of you. He then pours His prayers through you. They are His prayers—God-inspired, and hence, God answered (E. Stanley Jones, ***The Divine Yes***).

Prayer is learning to engage ourselves in the supernatural. Prayer is supernatural because it goes beyond the natural. We pray because we know that where we are, what we are facing, and what we have experienced will not change unless God breaks in. Therefore, we move from the natural to the supernatural for we are seeking God to do what we can't do. Prayer is the vehicle God uses to bring about His purpose, plan, and will. When we remove prayer from the equation, God's purpose, will, and strategy have no vehicle of transporting that to us.

The late J. Edwin Orr observed, "Whenever God is ready to do something new with His people, He always sets them to praying" (Wesley Campbell, ***Welcoming a Visitation of the Holy Spirit***).

Prayer changes us before it changes others. Prayer changes our perspective of self, others, and the world, and we begin to see things from God's viewpoint. Prayer is the most significant force in the world. It changes individuals, communities, nations, and yes, the world.

> Prayer is the most powerful force in the world because it invites Jesus into our midst. Prayer is the avenue the Lord has chosen to establish His reign and rule upon Planet Earth and in our lives. The very nature of prayer provokes change. Therefore, when we pray, we must be willing to change (Terry Teykl, ***The Presence Based Church***).

Praying from a kingdom perspective means God wants to show us something about Himself—something about His nature and character that causes us to want that in our lives and the lives of others. When we pray, "Your Kingdom come...on earth as it is in heaven" (Matthew 6:10), it means we desire what is in heaven to take place where we are. We are citizens of heaven—sons and daughters of God—for the kingdom of God is within us; we can know what is on the Father's heart that He desires for us to pray.

Prayer begins with God and ends with God. We become the conduit through which the kingdom of God is realized.

Evangelist Andrew Murray stated, "Jesus never taught His disciples how to preach, only how to pray. He did not speak much of what was needed to preach well, but much of praying well. Jesus loves to teach us to pray" (***God's Best Secrets***).

Let us come before the Lord in a childlike manner saying to Him, "Teach us to pray." I pray God will take us to a deep place in His heart as He teaches us to pray bold, audacious prayers that affect the world around us. Let us come boldly to the Lord to receive His heart and passion for the world as He teaches us to pray prayers that move mountains and change the trajectory of our lives and for those whom we pray. May the Lord fill you with the fullness of His Spirit as we pursue His presence through prayer.

Lesson 1

LORD, TEACH US TO PRAY

⌘

If there was one thing you would want Jesus to teach you, what would that be? The disciples of Jesus, observing His prayer life, came to Him and asked, "Lord, teach us to pray" (Luke 11:1). Why did they ask that question? Did they see something about His prayer life they desired for themselves? Did they see the relationship between what happened through Him as a direct result of what was happening in Him? The disciples took note of the long hours Jesus spent in prayer. They knew that He rose early in the morning to seek a private place in which to pray. They observed the intimacy He had with God, the Father. Jesus described His relationship with His heavenly Father this way, "The Son can do nothing of Himself, but what He sees the Father do; for whatever He does, the Son also does in like manner" (John 5:19). Since Jesus knew the importance of prayer, then we too must make prayer a priority.

The realization of our dependence upon the Lord is the dynamic that comes from our relationship with our heavenly Father. Therefore, we only do what we see and hear He is doing. Knowing and receiving the heart of God is what makes prayer so vital. Jesus knew the critical link to represent the Father's heart to the people was through prayer. Prayer for Jesus was the lifeline to release the kingdom of God upon the earth.

The prayer life of Jesus was the selfless act of giving Himself continuously to the will, plan, and purpose of God.

PRAYER FOR JESUS WAS THREEFOLD

• It was a place of **refreshing** to sustain spiritual effectiveness. "Now in the morning, having risen a long while before daylight, He went out and departed to a solitary place; and there He prayed" (Mark 1:35).

I find the morning is the most refreshing hour of the day. It is a time set aside to enjoy being with God only. Before the day gets cluttered with activity, I meet first with God to keep my spiritual effectiveness throughout the day and to be refreshed in my spirit. Meeting with God is not a duty to be performed, but a presentation of myself to Him (Romans 12:1).

• It was a place of **receiving** to stay focused on His purpose. Jesus said, "I don't speak on my own authority. The Father who sent me has commanded me what to say and how to say it" (John 12:49, NLT). Throughout the ministry of Jesus, both the enemy (the devil) and men sought to cause Him to deviate from His purpose and mission (Luke 4:1-13; John 6:15). Prayer for us is a place of receiving the heart and mind of God for the day.

Prayer is receiving our assignment from the Lord so that we can fulfill the purpose and mission of Jesus.

• It was a place of **revelation** to speak what was on the Father's heart (John 5:19). Jesus knew the importance of spiritual effectiveness. He knew the importance of staying focused on touching people at that point of need. He knew the importance of saying only those things the Father was speaking—to unveil the heart of God to those who needed to know His love and that He cared deeply for them.

He declares, "The words that I speak to you are spirit, and they are life" (John 6:63b). Time spent with God increases our ability to hear Him and to receive from Him the power to do what He has asked of us. Prayer is receiving the life-giving Words of Jesus so that we too can speak life-giving words that encourage, build up, and bring comfort.

We speak the revealed heart of God that carries words of healing and wholeness. We speak words that release the captive and words that bring comfort to the discouraged and hurting. Jesus made spending time with His heavenly Father a priority and so must we. We are to carry out the ministry of Jesus as He said we would (John 14:12).

POWERPOINT: Prayer for Jesus was more than an activity to be completed, but a place of meeting with His Father. Prayer for Jesus was a relationship to be cultivated with His heavenly Father. Prayer for Jesus was more than a ritual, but a place to receive the heart, the mind, and the assignment of His heavenly Father.

OBSERVATION: What made the prayer life of Jesus so powerful?

CHARACTERISTICS OF PRAYER

First of all, be bold. The writer of Hebrews encourages us to "come boldly to the throne of grace, that we may obtain mercy and find grace to help in time of need" (Hebrews 4:16). The word "bold" means frankness, sincerity, courage, and confidence.

We come boldly before the Father presenting our petitions and requests to Him knowing He will hear us and answer us.

Unfortunately, we may come to God thinking the opposite—that we are unworthy, or feel we don't have the right words to say, or that someone else can pray more powerfully than we can, or we feel we have disqualified ourselves by what has been said or done. But, we are to come boldly to God with the realization we are His sons and daughters. We come boldly before our heavenly Father and declare our need or the need of another with honesty, courage, and confidence. We come boldly not trusting in our goodness, but the goodness of God's amazing grace and His unfettered, unrestrained love.

The disciples found themselves in conflict with the religious rulers and elders of the day. The religious leaders demanded they do no more miracles, like the lame man who was now walking, leaping, and praising God (Acts 3:8).

The crippled man sat at the gate of the temple called the Beautiful Gate all his life. Peter encouraged the lame man to look at him, and he declared in the name of Jesus Christ to rise and walk (Acts 3:1-10). When the disciples heard the discouraging and disparaging words of the religious community not to preach, teach, or heal in the name of Jesus, they responded:

> "Now, Lord, look on their threats, and grant to Your servants that with all boldness they may speak Your word, by stretching out Your hand to heal, and that signs and wonders may be done through the name of Your holy Servant Jesus." And when they had prayed, the place where they were assembled together was shaken; and they were all filled with the Holy Spirit, and they spoke the word of God with boldness (Acts 4:29-31).

We need to see the connection between the disciples asking Jesus to teach them to pray, and how they watched Him speak words of healing, freedom, and restoration. Both through the example of Jesus and the power of the Holy Spirit, they could pray boldly, courageously, and expectantly. The key to praying bold, courageous prayers is spending time with our heavenly Father. Spending time with Him and getting to know His heart and mind creates in us a desire to pray bold, courageous, and powerful prayers that move mountains (Matthew 17:20).

To pray boldly means to:

- Know our identity in Christ (Romans 8:15-16).
- Pray the Word of God (Colossians 1:9-14).
- Learn to abide in Christ (John 15:5).
- Be confident the Spirit is helping us to pray (Romans 8:26-27).
- Know the Father's heart (John 17:20-26).
- Declare the Lord is our Helper (Hebrews 13:6).

POWERPOINT: May the Lord challenge us, stretch us, and embolden us to become powerful people of prayer. What happens **in** us is expressed **through** us. It becomes powerful, noticeable, and desirable.

The **second** characteristic of prayer is that it creates hunger. When we are in the presence of God, it creates a desire to be like Him, to know Him intimately, and to know His ways. Jesus said, "Blessed are those who hunger and thirst for righteousness [right relationship] for they shall be filled" (Matthew 5:6). The Psalmist describes his deep hunger for the presence of God, "O God, You are my God; early will I seek You; my soul thirsts for You; my flesh longs for You; in a dry and thirsty land where there is no water. So I looked for You in the sanctuary to see Your power and Your glory" (Psalm 63:1-2). Prayer provokes us out of complacency to create hunger, desire, and passion for more of Him. When we draw near to God, others begin to see our hunger and thirst for His presence in us. It leads others to desire to drink from the same fountain from which we drink deeply—His presence.

The more we pray, the more we want to pray. The more we want to pray, the more passionately we pray.

> The one defining characteristic that I believe to be the common denominator among Presence based pastors is humility. They have healthy desperation to know and understand the things of God and a deep yearning for His abiding Presence in their lives and churches (Terry Teykl, ***The Presence Based Church***).

The **third** characteristic of prayer is that it challenges us. When we draw near to God, we desire His presence. We pray with expectation, we pray more boldly, and we pray with greater conviction. Prayer challenges us to go beyond safe prayers and causes us to step out and to pray bold, audacious, and large prayers filled with faith (Hebrews 11:6). We are people of faith. Jesus said faith is the key to answered prayer, "I tell you, you can pray for anything, and if you believe that you've received it, it will be yours" (Mark 11:24, NLT). Prayer challenges our faith to believe God is greater than all our fears, all our doubts, and all our disappointments.

Prayer connects us to God in such a way we believe nothing is impossible with Him.

When we ask the Lord to "teach us to pray," He takes us to another level of prayer, a new posture from which to pray, and a new lens through which to see Him, others, and ourselves. He takes us to new paths of prayer, new ways of praying, and new experiences of joy in prayer. Thus, we are challenged to pray with a greater expectation. We will look more closely at expectation in the next chapter.

POWERPOINT: Prayer is not the reducing of God into our image, but the releasing of His mighty strength that comes from an abiding relationship with Him.

It is not so much that we get prayer, but that prayer gets us. It is the language of the heart that expresses deep gratitude to the One who knows us best. Prayer is more than a function we perform as believers. It is the positioning and posturing of our heart before God, and us reporting for duty.

The **fourth** characteristic of prayer is that it changes the atmosphere. The atmosphere in us affects the atmosphere around us. When the Lord is on the throne of our hearts, He is the One who calms the troubled waters around us.

When I speak of atmosphere, I am talking of the prevailing spirit that is within us. Either we have a prevailing spirit of fear, anxiety, and worry, or we have a prevailing spirit of peace, rest, and trust. Whatever prevailing spirit resides within us will affect the atmosphere around us.

When we speak from our fears, doubts, and unbelief, it is hard to pray powerfully, faithfully, and courageously.

For example, when Jesus and His disciples experienced a storm at sea and the disciples were afraid and called upon Jesus to help them and save them, Jesus looked squarely into the face of the storm and announced, "Peace, be still" (Mark 4:39). Though there was a great storm that surrounded them, Jesus spoke from that which filled Him —peace. When we go through trying times, because of Christ in us, we too have His peace, and we also can speak to those things that are going on around us that disturb or rob us of our peace.

We too can speak to the storms that surround us, "Peace, be still." We find yet another example of what happens around us when the peace of Christ fills our hearts with praise and worship as we look at Paul and Silas in prison. The atmosphere changed through their prayer and praise (Acts 16:25).

This atmospheric pressure charged with the power of the Holy Spirit opened prison doors to set the prisoners free, and the jailor and his family came to profess their faith in Christ (Acts 16:26-34). We are a people who can pray powerfully, and with confidence, as the power of Christ in us changes the atmosphere around us.

Changing the atmosphere begins with having a grateful heart—a heart filled with praise and thanksgiving. Paul and Silas began to shift their focus from themselves, their circumstances, and their confinement.

They acknowledged that the heavenly Father in their midst could do mighty things. They discovered freedom in their imprisonment. Their heart of prayer, praise, and worship came from the change God made in them. The atmosphere changed around them as the presence of the Lord was ushered in through prayer, praise, and worship. What God does in us is as powerful as what He does through us. Christ in us enables us to change the atmosphere from chaos to order, from disarray to peace, and from confusion to a sound mind.

What were the disciples asking when they said, "Lord, teach us to pray"?

- Teach us the joy of prayer, instead of the duty to pray.
- Teach us to make prayer a lifestyle, instead of an obligation to be fulfilled.

- Teach us new ways of praying, not just what we pray for all the time.
- Teach us to pray with greater expectation than what we are currently praying.
- Teach us to live so dependently upon You where anything that happens through us is because of You.
- Teach us not to limit You, but to release You, for nothing is impossible with You.

GROWTH POINT: Which of the six areas listed above are you asking God to grow?

IN SUMMARY

We advance the kingdom of God through prayer because the kingdom of God is a product of the nature and character of God. Wherever He is, we will find His Kingdom at work, yet it will take our pressing into what He desires to see it come to pass. What is it we want to see come to pass? Then we must pray for it to come to fruition and not give up until we see the reality of it. God has put His sons and daughters in charge of Planet Earth, and we are responsible for bringing the kingdom of God to be a present reality where we are.

The violent decision one must make to enter the kingdom of God is laying down everything that stands between us, God, and others.

Prayer ushers in the kingdom of God and is the key to unlocking the resources of heaven to work on our behalf. When we pray, our faith is released to believe God for the impossible. We are asking Him to awaken our spirits so that we can respond to His Spirit. We are declaring the manifest presence of God to be felt, experienced, known, and demonstrated. We come with confidence and with all boldness as the Lord invites us to draw near to Him. The Father delights to hear the voices of His sons and daughters. It is not about being worthy or unworthy to pray. It is about knowing the Father's heart and knowing how much He loves us. We learn to pray powerful prayers because we are His sheep, and His sheep hear His voice, and He leads us out (John 10:3).

LET'S TALK ABOUT IT

1. Review the questions in the lesson and discuss your responses.

2. How can prayer create spiritual hunger?

3. What prevents us from praying larger prayers?

4. What is your greatest challenge when it comes to prayer?

5. How can prayer impact the atmosphere around us?

6. What were the disciples asking when they said, "Lord, teach us to pray"?

7. What one thing can you take away from this lesson?

Lesson 2

LORD, LET YOUR KINGDOM COME

⌘

What are we asking the Lord to do when we say, "Your Kingdom come" (Luke 11:2)? How would this change the way we live and think? What makes this prayer so powerful? When we say "kingdom," we are speaking of the reign and rule of God. We are also talking about the characteristics that make up His kingdom: righteousness, peace, and joy in the Holy Spirit (Romans 14:17). We said in the previous lesson that prayer challenges us to move beyond where we are in our present prayer life to enter into a new dimension of prayer. We declare what is happening in heaven to be a present reality where we are. When we declare the kingdom of God to come and be a present reality in our lives and the lives of others, we pray with: confidence, assurance, authority, and boldness for we serve a great big God.

WHEN WE PRAY, "YOUR KINGDOM COME"

First of all, we pray in agreement. The early disciples were anticipating the promise from the Father about which Jesus had told them. They were to "stay here in the city until the Holy Spirit comes and fills you with power from heaven" (Luke 24:49, NLT). The Bible states, "These all continued with **one accord** in prayer" (Acts 1:14, emphasis added). The disciples agreed together that what Jesus told them would happen to them, in them, and through them. Though they did not know what to expect, all of their energy, time, and focus was to be in agreement with Jesus and powerful things would happen.

On the Day of Pentecost, "they were all with one accord in one place" (Acts 2:1). Jesus said, "I say to you that if two of you **agree** on earth concerning anything that they ask, it will be done for them by My Father in heaven" (Matthew 18:19, emphasis added).

The phrase "one accord" means to be in agreement, be in unity, and to have one mind and purpose. The word "agree" means to sound together—to be in harmony. It is where we get the word "symphony." The disciples were united in prayer, which means they were of one mind and heart ready to receive the gift of the Holy Spirit. This was like music to the Father's heart.

There was a symphony of agreeing prayer going to the Father that released the power of the Spirit that would rest upon the disciples.

The power of God is released:

- When we give ourselves to agree in prayer, it raises our expectation that God will move on our behalf (Psalm 62:5).
- When we offer ourselves to agree in prayer, our faith is stirred to believe nothing is impossible with God (Luke 1:37).
- When we give ourselves to agree in prayer, it fills us with a hope that cannot be shaken, for we have set our eyes on the God of hope (Romans 15:13).

- When we give ourselves to agree in prayer, we know that God "is able to do exceedingly abundantly above all that we ask or think according to the power that works in us" (Ephesians 3:20). Let us give ourselves to agreeing prayer and see what great things God will do.

GROWTH POINT: What makes agreeing prayer so powerful?

Second, we pray for transformation. Prayer affects the spiritual climate around us, and it touches the audience God has given to us. Paul writing to Timothy said, "I desire that men pray everywhere lifting up holy hands" (1 Timothy 2:8). Where is that spot, that place where God has put you? Begin to fill that place with the beautiful fragrance of Christ's love, and let Him change the spiritual climate.

POWERPOINT: If we want to change the order of the day, we must seek first the reign and rule of God to be in us. We serve an extraordinary God who does extraordinary things like signs, wonders, and miracles. We do not settle for what is normal, except the signs, wonders, and miracles are normal for the Christian life.

> Prayer is the agent that turns around what only the Lord can turn around. Prayer establishes fruit that will not be taken away. We can establish ourselves not only as people of prayer but also as a praying people. We cannot truly pray and remain the same. The very nature of prayer provokes change. Therefore, when we pray, we must be willing to change (Terry Teykl, ***The Presence Based Church***).

The kingdom of God is made up of transformed people. "Beloved, now we are children of God; and it has not yet been revealed what we shall be, but we know that when He is revealed, we shall be like Him, for we shall see Him as He is" (1 John 3:2). The Kingdom is made up of those who resemble Him, who take on the nature and character of Christ "because as He is, so are we in this world (1 John 4:17). We live as citizens of the kingdom of God.

LIVING AS TRANSFORMED PEOPLE

The world does not recognize us. We will be scoffed at, ridiculed, and mocked. Jesus explains why the world will misunderstand us. The Bible says, "The reason why the world does not know us is that it did not know Him" (1 John 3:1b, ESV). Jesus wants us to carry on His ministry when He said, "Truly, truly, I say to you, whoever believes in me will also do the works that I do; and greater works than these will he do, because I am going to the Father" (John 14:12, ESV). We should not be surprised that adversity comes our way and trials seek to disrupt our fellowship with Christ. God can take these things and use them to transform us into the likeness of Christ.

We seek a life that pleases and honors the Lord just as Jesus did with His heavenly Father. "And He who sent Me is with Me. The Father has not left Me alone, for I always do those things that please Him" (John 8:29). We are God's beloved sons and daughters in whom our heavenly Father is well pleased just as the Father affirms His Son, Jesus, "This is My beloved Son, in whom I am well pleased" (Matthew 3:17b).

We live in union with God through Christ. "But he who is joined to the Lord is one spirit with Him" (1 Corinthians 6:17). We live as transformed people in a world that desperately needs an encounter with the living Christ.

We have God's Spirit living in us that identifies us as His sons and daughters created in His likeness.

We are continuously transformed into the image of Christ as Paul describes, "But we all, with unveiled face, beholding as in a mirror the glory of the Lord, are being **transformed** into the same image from glory to glory, just as the Spirit of the Lord" (2 Corinthians 3:18, emphasis added). Transformation takes place when we surrender to God's goodness and say "yes" to His best.

"To pray is to change. Prayer is the central avenue God uses to transform us. If we are unwilling to change, we will abandon prayer as a noticeable characteristic of our lives" (Richard Foster, ***Celebration of Discipline***).

The disciples waited in expectation to receive the gift of the Holy Spirit that would transform their lives from the inside out. They would become bold, powerful witnesses to Jesus Christ and to the transformation that He promised to give to all who received His Spirit.

Prayer is the relinquishment of ourselves to God allowing Him to transform us into the image of His Son, Jesus.

Third, we pray with expectation. We expect when we pray that the Lord hears what we are saying. We look to Him to speak to us about how we are to pray. We receive His agenda, and we pray till it comes to pass. We know God will provide, intervene, direct, empower, and equip us to receive that for which we are praying. The missing ingredient in many of our prayers is an expectation accompanied by faith.

To pray with expectation:

- Is to be filled with hope (Romans 5:5; 15:13; Hebrews 10:23).
- Is to be filled with confidence (Ephesians 3:12; Hebrews 10:35).
- Is to be filled with faith (Hebrews 11:1, 6; Romans 10:17).
- Is to wait patiently upon the Lord (Psalm 62:5; Romans 8:19).
- Is to lay aside weariness and defeat (Galatians 6:9; 1 Corinthians 15:58; 2 Corinthians 4:16).
- Is to know that the Lord is good (Psalm 34:8; James 1:17).

OBSERVATION: Why is it essential we pray with expectation?

If we have no expectation, why would we pray? The very reason we can pray with expectation is that the Spirit of the living God lives in us.

> May the God of hope fill you with all joy and peace in believing [through the experience of your faith] that by the power of the Holy Spirit you will abound in hope and overflow with confidence in His promises (Romans 15:13, AMP).

We pray because we have set our hope upon God who is "able to [carry out His purpose and] do superabundantly more than all that we dare ask or think [infinitely beyond our greatest prayers, hopes, or dreams], according to His power that is at work within us" (Ephesians 3:20, AMP).

POWERPOINT: Our expectation can change the spiritual climate around us—from hopelessness to hope-filled, from lethargy to fullness of life, from despair to cheerfulness, and from being unaware of God's activity among His people to a greater awareness of His presence.

I was putting the final touches for my Sunday morning message one Saturday evening, and these words began to form in my mind, "We are not to be conditioned to accept things as unchangeable." I was preaching on the woman who had been hemorrhaging for years and spent all she had, only to get worse (Luke 8:40-48). Her objective was to touch the hem of Jesus' garment, and she knew she would receive her healing (Mark 5:28).

The sincere desire of this woman, and the desperate plight she found herself was not conditioned to accept things as unchangeable. Her change happened because she was not conditioned to accept things as unchangeable. So let's remove all the things we have been conditioned to accept in our lives as unchangeable.

We serve a mighty God, and with Him nothing is impossible. We expect great things and nothing less will do.

Fourth, we pray with a desire. When we pray, "Let Your Kingdom come," we pray with a great desire to see His presence manifested among us. We know it is the Father's good pleasure to give us the Kingdom (Luke 12:32).

His desire becomes our desire to see His kingdom manifested, made known to us, in ways that bring honor and glory to His name. Jesus said, "Therefore I say to you, whatever things you ask [desire] when you pray, believe that you receive them, and you will have them" (Mark 11:24). Our desire is for Him.

The Psalmist expresses his passion, "One thing I have desired of the Lord, that will I seek: That I may dwell in the house of the Lord all the days of my life, to behold the beauty of the Lord, and to inquire in His temple" (Psalm 27:4). The desire is for His presence to be known. We desire to behold His glory, splendor, and how awesome He is. We want heaven to come down. It is a heart surrendered to Christ that seeks to see the kingdom of God ruling and reigning upon Planet Earth and His glory to cover the earth as the waters cover the sea (Habakkuk 2:14).

The kingdom of God is made known to those who have found in Christ all they need, all they want, and all they desire.

We desire that Jesus would make Himself known in and through us. We are His vessels, instruments through which the kingdom of God becomes a present reality where we are.

With all our shortcomings and imperfections, we are jars of clay through which God has chosen to demonstrate His power and glory (Romans 9:21).

We minister from fullness, not a partial Jesus, or an incomplete Jesus, or a just barely enough Jesus.

We live in a completeness that comes from Christ living in us for He desires to express Himself through us to the world.

Father, give us a greater hunger for Your presence, a greater desire to demonstrate Your love, a greater passion for experiencing Your freedom, and a greater boldness to present You anew and afresh to those around us.

Fifth, we pray with vision. Paul's prayer for the church at Ephesus was that the eyes of their heart would be enlightened (Ephesians 1:18). That is, he wanted us to know the greatness of the hope we have in Jesus Christ, to see the goodness of the nature and character of God, and to see the extravagance of His love. The Father wants us to live through eyes of faith (2 Corinthians 5:7).

The Lord wants to awaken our eyes to see from another dimension. We live from our five senses (sight, smell, hearing, taste, and touch). God gives us another dimension from which to view life—it is through His eyes.

ELISHA PRAYS FOR HIS SERVANT (2 Kings 6:13-17)

To see through God's eyes, we must **first** look from His perspective. When Elisha's servant saw the tremendous

Syrian army that surrounded them, he was overcome with fear, "Alas, my master! What shall we do?" (2 Kings 6:15). Elisha's servant was unable to see things through the lens of God's perspective. He could only see the vast number of soldiers that surrounded them.

Our heavenly Father wants us to have a revelation of seeing things from His perspective through His greatness and goodness. John exhorts us to see from God's perspective, "You are of God, little children, and have overcome them because He who is in you is greater than he who is in the world" (1 John 4:4). It is through prayer God opens the eyes of our heart and allows us to see things from His perspective. This young man could not see; fear had clouded his vision and his ability to understand that God in the midst of them is mighty.

Elisha reassured his servant, "Do not fear, for those who are with us are more than those who are with them" (2 Kings 6:16). The Father's answer to fear is that "there is no fear in love; but perfect love casts out fear, because fear involves torment. But he who fears has not been made perfect in love" (1 John 4:18). We all need the assurance that God in the midst of us is mighty and gives us the power to overcome whatever the enemy throws at us. We need a revelation of how much God loves us for it changes the way we see things.

Fear is the great robber of our spiritual vision that keeps us from fully trusting the Father and His ability to handle any problem that comes our way. Jesus did not come to torment us. He came to destroy the one who does torment us—the devil—with tormenting thoughts that disturb us, distract us, and distress us. Jesus came to give us His peace and to assure us of His presence.

Second, to see through God's eyes, we must open our eyes to the unseen. Elisha prayed for his servant, "Lord, I pray, open his eyes that he may see" (2 Kings 6:17a). Prayer is what enables us to see into another dimension we are unable to see with our physical eyes. Paul said, "We walk by faith, not by sight" (2 Corinthians 5:7). Faith takes us into another dimension, a new level of living, we had not known before. Elisha's servant was stepping into that dimension. To have our eyes awakened means our faith has been awakened to see things from God's perspective—His point of view—for His ways are higher than ours (Isaiah 55:9).

May we have eyes to see into the supernatural realm of God's Spirit. God answered Elisha's prayer for his servant, "Then the Lord opened the eyes of the young man, and he saw. And behold, the mountain was full of chariots of fire all around Elisha" (2 Kings 6:17b).

May we have our eyes opened to behold the Lord of glory in all His beauty, splendor, and greatness.

To behold is to look to Jesus, the Author and Finisher of our faith (Hebrews 12:2). We are looking away from everything else that might distract us from beholding the Lord of glory. May our eyes be opened to the truth of God's Word as the Psalmist asks, "Open my eyes, that I may see wondrous things from Your law" (Psalm 119:18).

When we walk in the truth of God's Word, it gives us insight to live in victory and wisdom for daily living.

Let me illustrate what I mean. Two disciples were walking on the road to Emmaus following the crucifixion of Jesus and encountered a stranger. He inquired what they were discussing. Unknown to them, this stranger was Jesus, and He explained the Scriptures speaking about the Messiah. When the disciples reached their destination, they invited Him to have supper with them. When Jesus was breaking the bread, He suddenly left their presence, and they declared to one another, "Did not our heart burn within us while He talked with us on the road, and while He opened the Scriptures to us?" (Luke 24:32). When the eyes of our heart open to the truth of God's Word, it releases wisdom, equips us to live an overcoming life, and liberates us for joyful obedience.

POWERPOINT: *Father, give us a greater hunger for Your presence. A great desire to demonstrate Your love. A greater passion for experiencing Your freedom and a greater boldness to present You anew and afresh to those around us.*

Third, to see through God's eyes, we live in the light of His truth. We know we are children of the light because the Light of the World is living in us, and we shine brightly because of Him. We no longer are people of darkness alienated from God, living with selfish motives, living at cross-purposes with God. Paul describes this way of living as "following the course of this world, following the prince of the power of the air, the spirit that is now at work in the sons of disobedience" (Ephesians 2:2b, ESV).

We no longer live by the standards of this world, but the standards of the kingdom of God, "For you were once darkness, but now you are light in the world. Walk as children of light" (Ephesians 5:8). God commands His sons and daughters to "walk as children of light." The next verses describe what it means to walk as children of the light, "(For the fruit of light is found in all that is good and right and true), and try to discern what is pleasing to the Lord" (Ephesians 5:9-10, ESV).

Jesus declared, "While you have the light, believe in the light, that you may become sons of light" (John 12:36). Paul writes, "We are all children of the light, children of the day. We are not of the night or of the darkness" (1 Thessalonians 5:5, ESV). Jesus describes the sons of the kingdom as "the righteous will shine forth as the sun in the kingdom of their Father" (Matthew 13:43). From these truths, we are people of the Light shining brightly the love of Jesus to the world and demonstrating kingdom living as transformed people.

IN SUMMARY

We pray that God would stretch us in our prayer life—that He would take us from the ordinary to the extraordinary, from the seen to the unseen, from natural to the supernatural, from defeat to overcoming. May the Lord open the eyes of our heart that we might know the things freely given to us by Him (1 Corinthians 2:12). May the kingdom of God become a present reality as the Lord takes us from glory to glory.

LET'S TALK ABOUT IT

1. What difference does it make when we pray with expectation?

2. What does it mean to pray with desire?

3. What does it mean to pray with spiritual vision?

4. In 2 Kings 6:13-17, what kept Elisha's servant from seeing? What did Elisha do that helped this young man see?

5. Why must we see from God's perspective?

6. What does it mean to live in the light of God's truth?

7. What are you asking the Father to do as a result of this lesson?

Lesson 3

Prayer Releases the Kingdom of God

⌘

In Paul's letter to the church at Colossae while imprisoned at Rome around 62 A.D., he encouraged the church to "Devote yourselves to prayer" (Colossians 4:2, NLT). What does it mean to be devoted to prayer? Does this imply a lifestyle of prayer? The word "devote" means to concentrate on a particular pursuit or purpose and in this case, prayer.

Paul illustrates his point concerning "devoted prayer"as he writes, "Epaphras, a member of your own fellowship and a servant of Christ Jesus, sends you his greetings. He always prays **earnestly** for you, asking God to make you strong and perfect, fully confident that you are following the whole will of God" (Colossians 4:12, NLT, emphasis added). The word "earnest" means to continue to be vigilant, watchful, to give strict attention. We find that these words "devoted" and "earnest" communicate the same idea, the kind of prayer that is dedicated and intensive.

Let me paraphrase Colossians 4:2: *Let our prayer be filled with purpose as we pursue the whole will and counsel of God in all things. Be vigilant and not passive in our prayer life and give attention to it from which the presence of God flows to you and through you.*

Prayer releases God to do mighty things that we cannot do on our own. It releases all of heaven to bring healing, deliverance, and restoration. Prayer is powerful, and we are called to release this power upon the earth. Jesus encouraged His disciples to be constant in prayer and never to give up. Jesus describes in the parable of the widow the need for persistent, earnest prayer (Luke 18:1-8). This widow illustrates the need for persistent, determined prayer with the resolve not to give up when needing a breakthrough. We must pray earnestly.

INGREDIENTS THAT RELEASE THE KINGDOM OF GOD

First of all, you release the kingdom of God by having a mindset toward prayer. Paul writes, "Your attitude should be the same that Christ Jesus had" (Philippians 2:5, NLT). Jesus' attitude was one of complete dependence and obedience to His heavenly Father. Jesus only did what He saw His Father doing. Jesus said, "I assure you, the Son can do nothing by Himself. He does only what He sees the Father doing. Whatever the Father does, the Son also does" (John 5:19, NLT). We are to live with the same attitude and mindset as Jesus.

Prayer is connecting with God and expressing our dependence upon Him and our need to walk in obedience to what he is saying and doing. Jesus described it this way, "I am the vine; you are the branches. Those who remain in me, and I in them, will produce much fruit. For apart from me you can do nothing" (John 15:5, NLT). We, too, receive our life from Jesus for we have attached ourselves to Him.

POWERPOINT: Prayer is like spiritual breathing. We breathe in—inhale the life of God as we welcome Him into all areas of our life. We exhale—we breathe out by surrendering ourselves to Him, only to breathe in His presence once again.

Second, to release the kingdom of God, we must have a commitment to pray. Prayer releases the resources of the kingdom of God and the key to unlocking the resources of heaven to work on our behalf. When we pray, our faith is being released to believe God for the impossible. We are asking Him to awaken our spirit to respond to His Spirit. We declare the manifest glory of God to be felt, experienced, and known. Prayer opens heaven's door to heal the brokenhearted, to set the captive free, and to know the saving grace of God. Prayer allows us to stand under an open heaven—to know and receive the things freely given to us by God (1 Corinthians 2:10-12). This is the fruit of committing ourselves to prayer.

> Real change and transformation come through a commitment to radical prayer. We are not just committed to another program, but committed to cultivating a relationship with Jesus (Michael Slaughter, ***Unlearning Church***).

Prayer is the access point to releasing the resources of heaven.

It is living in the truth that we are seated with Christ in heavenly places (Ephesians 2:6). We live from this truth that we are seated with Christ in the heavenly places; we release the presence of God, His kingdom, and the very sounds of heaven upon the earth. We walk in the realm of the supernatural, knowing God can break in and release miracles, the long-awaited breakthrough, and the sincere desires of the heart.

- It releases life where dreams, hopes, and aspirations have been lost, forgotten, or forsaken.
- It releases hope where there has been hopelessness, despair, and emptiness.
- It releases joy that brings strength when we feel weak, abandoned, and forgotten.
- It releases His presence that infuses us with eyes to see, ears to hear, and hearts to respond.
- It releases the light of His glory in the midst of darkness, fear, despair, discouragement, and failure.

POWERPOINT: May the Lord open the storehouse of heaven, that displays the splendor of His glory, and majesty, where we experience the extravagance of His love, and encounter the One who meets us at our point of need (Philippians 4:19).

Third, to release the kingdom of God, we must have the persistence to pray. There is power in retelling the story of how God makes a way when there seems to be no way. In all places of life, whether good times or tough times, we need to hear the story again and again that gives us hope, promise, and victory.

We need to be reminded of whose we are, that God is God, and there is none like Him. Remember that the One who saved us is also the One who delivers and keeps us.

King Herod Agrippa had just killed James, the brother of John, the first of the twelve disciples to be martyred. He also put Peter in prison to possibly face the same death while guards watched over him. We see that God made a way when there seemed to be no way to escape from Herod, "So when he had arrested him, he put him in prison, and delivered him to four squads of soldiers to keep him" (Acts 12:4). Herod wanted to silence the message and the messenger. We find that the church persistently prayed for Peter during his incarceration. "So Peter was kept in prison, but earnest prayer for him was made to God by the church" (Acts 12:5, ESV). God stirred up the heart of the church to pray for Peter's life, his protection, and his release. It was this kind of earnest prayer that brought deliverance and freedom to him.

This kind of intense, earnest prayer also describes the level of prayer Jesus prayed in Gethsemane. "And being in agony, He prayed more earnestly" (Luke 22:44). The prayer of Jesus in the Garden also describes the kind of high-level, intensive prayer the church had entered into for God to move on Peter's behalf.

The church earnestly prayed together believing God for a breakthrough for Peter, for God to intervene on his behalf, and that God would demonstrate His power to deliver. The church was not just going through the formality of prayer. It was Spirit-led and Spirit-empowered prayer that led to Peter's freedom.

The problem was their prayer was not mixed with expectation or faith. The church said to Rhoda when she told them Peter was at the door knocking, "You are beside yourself" (Acts 12:15a)! And when those who had been praying opened the door and saw that it was Peter, "they were astonished" (Acts 12:16b).

POWERPOINT: The truth is we can pray devoted and earnest prayers, but if prayer is not mixed with expectation and faith it only leads to frustration, disappointment, and disillusionment.

We are a people of faith, and we pray devoted, earnest prayers mixed with expectation and filled with faith.

Fourth, we release the kingdom of God when we have the peace of God. Peter was miraculously delivered from the confinement of prison, the chains that bound him, and from the soldiers that guarded him. Before Herod sent word to bring Peter out of prison to make a public spectacle out of him, we see, "And when Herod was about to bring him out, that night Peter was sleeping, bound with two chains between two soldiers; and the guards before the door were keeping the prison" (Acts 12:6).

Amid uncertainty, not knowing what lay before him, Peter was at complete rest and peace. Jesus said:

> Come to Me, all you who labor and are heavy laden, and I will give you rest. Take My yoke upon you and learn from Me, for I am gentle and lowly in heart, and you will find rest for your souls. For My yoke is easy and My burden is light (Matthew 11:28-30).

The words of Jesus describe an invitation from Him to come as we are with all our burdens, things that hold us down, the things that distract us, and the things that rob us of our strength and peace. Christ is inviting us to come and find our place of rest in Him, for the promise is "I will give you rest" which means He is our Source of rest; rest comes from Him. The key to this promise is the realization of our deep need for Christ.

To have the peace of God means:

- We trust the Lord to work all things together for our good and His glory (Romans 8:28).
- We allow God to accomplish His purpose in our lives (Philippians 1:6) for it is a good work.
- We watch how the Lord works on our behalf to do in us and through us what we cannot do. "For our light affliction, which is but for a moment, is working for us a far more exceeding and eternal weight of glory" (2 Corinthians 4:17).
- We fix our eyes upon Jesus and not the problems that surround us (Hebrews 12:2).
- We declare the promises of God to come to pass as we stand upon the Word of God. "But the word of the Lord endures forever" (1 Peter 1:25). The "word" (rhema) is God's life-giving word for that moment, that season, that word to stand upon—a now word.
- We wait until our change comes as we enter into new realms of prayer, praise, and worship (Job 14:14; Philippians 4:6).

When we set our hearts to rest, trust the Lord, and watch His promises come to pass, the blessing finds its place of rest in Him. Do we want to live a blessed life? Then let us enter into God's rest. "Let us therefore be diligent to enter that rest" (Hebrews 4:11a). The phrase "be diligent" means to exert oneself, to make every effort, and to strain every nerve. We make rest a priority. Peter experienced the rest of God in his time of confinement. He discovered that in rest God makes a way of escape—the way of overcoming. Peter knew this kind of rest for He experienced it in the life of Jesus. We are finding the benefit, necessity, and blessing of earnest, devoted prayer.

PARDON THE INTERRUPTION

During a great storm at sea, we find Jesus "in the stern, asleep on a pillow. And they awoke Him and said to Him, 'Teacher, do You not care that we are perishing?'" (Mark 4:38). Peter learned from this experience that God watches over us, cares for us, and will deliver us out of circumstances beyond our control.

When going through the storms of life in uncertain times, we can find our place of rest and peace in Christ alone. The Psalmist tells us to "rest in the Lord, and wait patiently for Him" (Psalm 37:7).

Fifth, we have supernatural provision to release the kingdom of God. While Peter was resting in the Lord in a deep sleep, we find God is about to work on his behalf and the behalf of a praying church. "Now behold, an angel of the Lord stood by him, and a light shone in the prison; and he struck Peter on the side and raised him up, saying, 'Arise quickly!' And his chains fell off his hands" (Acts 12:7). The angel struck Peter on the side to awaken him out of the deep sleep. It was not a small, casual wake up call. It was something one could feel and demanded a response. God was getting Peter's attention because He was about to do something miraculous and undeniable.

The undeniable evidence that this was God:

- Chains fell off without using keys.
- Instructions from the angel for Peter to get dressed.
- Passing by the prison guards who were soundly asleep.
- Iron gates that were once locked are now open.
- The confirming words of Peter, "Now I know for certain that the Lord has sent His angel, and has delivered me from the hand of Herod" (Acts 12:11).

These five ingredients are the fruit of faithful, earnest prayer for Peter's release which resulted in many hearing and responding to the power of Jesus Christ for "the Word of God grew and multiplied" (Acts 12:24).

POWERPOINT: God causes the increase. When we think it is all over, God is not yet finished and has more to do in us and through us. Instead of looking for a human solution, we look for God's answer.

What does this mean to us?

- There are times God moves so miraculously that we can't believe our eyes. "But they [the church] said to her, 'You are beside yourself'" (Acts 12:15).
- We make excuses why something can't happen. "Yet she kept insisting that it was so. So they said, 'It is his angel'" (Acts 12:15).
- We may be surprised and astonished to see our prayers answered. "Now Peter continued knocking; and when they opened the door and saw him, they were astonished" (Acts 12:16).

- The enemy is confused. "Then, as soon as it was day, there was no small stir among the soldiers about what had become of Peter" (Acts 12:18).

GROWTH POINT: In which of these four areas are you asking God to strengthen you?

Whenever the church experiences testing or adversity, we have an opportunity to devote ourselves to prayer that brings forth the supernatural activity of God. Peter understood this truth that apart from Christ he could do nothing. Even in weakness, he discovered the power of Christ to be resident within him and activated it through faith. Peter's life of fruitfulness was a result of how he made the Lord his Source in the place of rest. When we find ourselves in that proverbial place "between a rock and a hard place," God will see us through. He will not forsake us or leave us without help. Just as God moved on Peter's behalf, He will do the same for us. The thing that moves the hand of God is persistent, devoted prayer mixed with believing faith.

May the Lord give us a faith to believe that even in the worst of circumstance, when our faith is challenged beyond what we feel we can endure, we would lean into God in such a way we find our place of rest and peace in Him alone.

LET'S TALK ABOUT IT

1. What is our attitude toward prayer to be?

2. According to Michael Slaughter, to what are we to commit ourselves to get real change and transformation?

3. What does it mean to pray with persistence?

4. How did the church's commitment to pray affect Peter's life? What did their prayer enable him to do?

5. According to Acts 12:24, what resulted from the church's prayers?

6. What is the key to a fruitful life?

7. What one thing are you taking away from this lesson?

Lesson Four

Prevailing Prayer

⌘

Let's continue to look at the prayer life of Epaphras whom Paul uses to illustrate devoted, earnest, and prevailing prayer.

> Epaphras, a member of your own fellowship and a servant of Christ Jesus, sends you his greetings. He always prays earnestly for you, asking God to make you strong and perfect, fully confident that you are following the whole will of God. I can assure you that he prays hard for you and also for the believers in Laodicea and Hierapolis (Colossians 4:12-13, NLT).

The truth is, we need someone who goes before God on our behalf. We need someone in our lives who prays for us prayers that make a difference. Do you have someone in your life who does that? In whose life are you making a difference by your prayers?

John Wesley made this bold statement about prayer:

> Give me 100 preachers who fear nothing but sin and desire nothing but God, and I care not a straw whether they be clergy or layman, such alone will shake the gates of hell and set up the Kingdom of

> heaven on earth. God does nothing but in answer to prayer.

There are some places we come to in life where the only way we stand is on our knees before the Lord.

Prayer is not the reducing of God into our image, but the releasing of the mighty strength that comes from an abiding relationship with Him.

THE POWER OF PREVAILING PRAYER

First of all, prevailing prayer keeps us amid temptation and opposition. Paul helps us to see the power of Christ in us is greater than what the devil or humanity may throw at us. Paul writes:

> No temptation has overtaken you except such as is common to man; but God is faithful, who will not allow you to be tempted beyond what you are able, but with the temptation will also make the way of escape, that you may be able to bear [endure] it (1 Corinthians 10:13).

Epaphras prays for the believers in Colossae to live an overcoming life: to resist the temptation to give up too soon, to settle for less than God's best, and to stand firm against the winds of adversity that would seek to blow them off course. We realize deception is a tool of the enemy, and we are not to be ignorant of his devices and schemes for he is the father of lies (John 8:44). His strategy is to keep us from living an overcoming, victorious, and prevailing life in Christ.

Second, prevailing prayer leads to spiritual maturity. Paul explains the goal of all ministry, "Him we proclaim, warning everyone and teaching everyone with all wisdom, that we may present everyone mature in Christ (Colossians 1:28, ESV). Epaphras prays that the church would be fruitful and walk in a maturity of faith that believes God works all things together for our good and His glory.

Minister and author Chuck Pierce explains the importance of spiritual maturity, "You must get to a place of maturity where you display who you are and are used to change or influence the culture you are positioned in for your future" (***Time to Defeat the Devil)***.

Living a Spirit-empowered life means we leave behind those things that hinder our spiritual growth and maturity. Therefore, we renounce old ways of thinking and believing that work against the purposes of God for our lives, our families, and our futures. We replace them with the truth of God's Word: the truth of who He is, the truth of who He says we are, the truth of what He says we can do, and the truth of what He says we can have. We bind our mind to the mind of Christ so that we will have His thoughts. "It was for this freedom that Christ set us free [completely liberating us]; therefore keep standing firm and do not be subject again to a yoke of slavery [which you once removed]" (Galatians 5:1, AMP). God's call upon our lives is spiritual maturity. One of the ways God designed to grow us toward spiritual maturity is through prevailing prayer. It is learning to prevail over the enemy, over strongholds, over discouraging thoughts, and everything else that would keep us from living an overcoming, victorious life through Jesus Christ. God has given us His Spirit to enable us, to empower us for such a lifestyle. Paul explains it this way, we walk by the Spirit and obey the Spirit's voice "if we live in the Spirit, let us also walk in the Spirit" (Galatians 5:25).

Third, prevailing prayer keeps us walking confidently in the Lord. Paul, in his letter to the church at Colossae, prays for their maturity and for them to walk confidently in the whole counsel of God. "Asking God to make you strong and perfect [mature], fully confident that you are following the whole will of God" (Colossians 4:12, NLT). In his letter to the Ephesians, Paul expresses it this way, "Then Christ will make His home in your hearts as you trust in him. Your roots will grow down into God's love and keep you strong" (Ephesians 3:17, NLT). Epaphras prays that believers remain faithful in the midst of adversity, hardship, and difficulty and that God would make them more than conquerors and cause them to walk confidently as mighty men and women of God.

The entire letter to the Colossians is about maturity filled with the fullness of Christ, "Him we preach, warning every man and teaching every man all wisdom, that we may present every man perfect [mature] in Christ Jesus" (Colossians 1:28, NIV). God has begun a good work in us toward spiritual maturity. This maturity enables us to walk confidently as sons and daughters of God.

Finally, prevailing prayer keeps us in the midst of spiritual warfare. Paul writes to the church at Ephesus about spiritual warfare,

> For we do not wrestle against flesh and blood, but against principalities, powers, against the rulers of

> the darkness of this age, against spiritual hosts of wickedness in the heavenly places. Therefore take up the whole armor of God, that you may be able to withstand in the evil day, and having done all, to stand" (Ephesians 6:12-13).

We will address more about spiritual warfare in lesson twelve.

Epaphras prays that the believers be aware of the ploys, plots, and plans of the enemy to make them ineffective in their witness before an unbelieving world. Paul states we need to be aware that there is a real devil, and he does not like us and will do anything to break our fellowship with Jesus. Paul addresses this issue as he explains, "In order that Satan might not outwit [take advantage of] us. For we are not unaware of his schemes [devices]" (2 Corinthians 2:11, NIV). We are to understand that the devil does not want us to succeed or grow in our spiritual lives. His goal is to keep us defeated and discouraged. Therefore, we must be aware of his tactics and not fall into the enemy's traps.

GROWTH POINT: How can prevailing prayer make a difference in your life?

God had called Epaphras to stand in the gap and to pray for the church at Colosse to be an overcoming church. His job was to pray a wall of protection that would fortify them from man's attempt to weaken their faith, from the enemy—the devil—who would seek to fill their minds with lies and deception, and from the world that would entice them to settle for second best instead of God's best.

Our prayer is that God would raise a person or persons who will stand in the gap before the Lord on behalf of the people of God and for the advancement of His Kingdom. Would He call us to be among these people?

FOUR INGREDIENTS TO PREVAILING PRAYER

First of all, prevailing prayer declares we are a people of vision. "Where there is no vision (no revelation of God and His Word), the people are unrestrained" (Proverbs 29:18, AMP). Our prayer is that God would open the eyes of our heart that we may see. The Holy Spirit awakens our spiritual vision so we can see the kingdom of God at work and pray for His Kingdom to come with power and glory.

Spiritual vision means:

- To see Christ in all His splendor and glory, mighty to help in time of trouble.
- To see Christ high and lifted above the chaos of the day.
- To see Him in His beauty and radiance in challenging times.

"God seeks to commune with you, to confirm His Word to your spirit, to inspire you to do great and mighty things, and to impart courage, faith, and new vision to you" (Frank Damazio, ***The Attitude of Faith).***

Second, prevailing prayer declares we are a people of the Spirit. We become His instruments attuned to His voice and walking in the Spirit as He fills us continuously with His Spirit (Ephesians 5:18).

THE SPIRIT COMES AS RAIN

When I was young, the youth group from our church was attending a conference, Camp Farthest Out, where we heard about the baptism of the Holy Spirit. Following one of the evening meetings, we prayed and asked to be filled with the Holy Spirit. We received this wonderful baptism in the Holy Spirit, and our hearts were filled with the love of God. Everyone in the youth group went outside the place we were lodging to sing, to shout, and to praise God for the wonderful encounter we had. The love of God filled our hearts with praise and thanksgiving. As we were singing and worshiping the Lord, a gentle rain began to fall confirming God's refreshing, renewing, and the pouring out of His Spirit upon us—we would never be the same. That night we were surprised by the overwhelming sense that we belonged to God and that He belonged to us.

That encounter ruined us for the ordinary, the mundane, the predictable, and God launched us into a new way of living called the supernatural lifestyle.

> Jesus was not into building programs, technology, media, or megachurches. He was about the business of empowering people to seek the lost, strengthen the weak, heal the sick, bind up the injured, and bring back those who had strayed. Not a program, but a radical demonstration of the power of God (Michael Slaughter, ***Unlearning Church***).

Third, prevailing prayer declares we are a people of the Word, and we embrace the Word of Life. Jesus became flesh and blood and dwelt among us (John 1:14). When the eyes of our heart open to the truth of God's Word, it releases wisdom, equips us to live overcoming lives, and liberates us for joyful obedience.

"The Word of God comes to us and stirs us to higher expectation—to believe what God says will come to pass." (Frank Damazio, ***The Attitude of Faith***).

Let the Word of God speak to the deepest part of who we are. Speaking to the desires of the heart, the hopes, and dreams we have. Let our times with the Lord be times of renewing, refreshing, and receiving a fresh word from which to live victoriously.

Fourth, prevailing prayer makes us a people of worship by drawing near to Christ. We give Christ His rightful place of honor and glory by submitting our lives to Him (John 4:24). In the presence of Christ, we all stand in His grace and power that prevails over all that the enemy would throw at us. The devil seeks to condemn, accusing us, telling us how bad we are, or reminding us of all our failures. To his lies, we must say, "No!" We will not believe what the enemy says about us for it is all lies; there is no truth in him (John 8:44). We stand in Christ forgiven, loved, freed, healed, delivered, and victorious.

WORSHIP TOUCHES THE FATHER'S HEART

God wants us to know His heart, and apart from spending time with Him, we will never know His deepest desires. The Father desires to spend time with His kids—His sons, and daughters. Time spent with God touches the Father's heart with our love, affection, and worship. The one desire of our hearts should be to please the Father, not through our efforts, but through our time with Him and giving ourselves to Him fully and freely. We say, "Come, Lord, Jesus" as we learn to prevail in prayer.

IN SUMMARY

The ability to pray with power is to know that I am a child of God, I have been born into the kingdom of God. I know that I am an heir of God and a joint-heir of Jesus Christ. I know that my position is not because of my goodness, but because of Christ's righteousness in me.

We can pray with power not because of our name, but in the name of the One to whom we belong. We can invoke His name and know His presence, His power, His provision, His pardon, and His pleasure. Prevailing prayer makes a difference and impacts the world around us. Let us prevail in prayer until we see the kingdom of God advancing upon the earth.

LET'S TALK ABOUT IT

1. Review the questions in the lesson and discuss your responses.

2. What does it mean to wrestle in prayer?

3. What does prevailing prayer mean to you?

4. What are the four ingredients to prevailing prayer? Which one spoke to you the most and why?

5. What is the purpose of prevailing prayer?

6. What does this statement mean: Prayer is not the reducing of God into our image, but the releasing of the mighty strength that comes from an abiding relationship with Him?

7. What are you asking the Father to do as a result of this lesson?

Lesson 5

Persevering Prayer Releases the Power of God

⌘

The disciples are left to wait for the promise Jesus said the Father would send in His name—to empower, to equip, and to establish them as authentic witnesses of the transforming power of Jesus Christ (Acts 1). These were pivotal days in the lives of those who followed Jesus as they waited for the promise of the Father to pour out His Spirit in a convincing manner.

RELEASING THE POWER OF GOD

First of all, we release the power of God through persevering prayer. Jesus' instruction to His disciples was to wait for the promise of the Father to send another Helper, the Holy Spirit. The Holy Spirit would reside in them and empower them to continue the ministry of Jesus (John 14:12). The disciples prepared themselves for this promise. Luke writes, "All these with one mind and one purpose were continually devoting themselves to prayer [waiting together]..." (Acts 1:14, AMP).

There is something powerful that happens and is released when God's people bombard heaven with constant, passionate prayer.

Persevering prayer is needed when answers do not come easy or when they get delayed. I liken this to a bulldog spirit that says, "I will not give up until my breakthrough comes." It is saying, "I will not give into the enemy's tactics to draw me off course from God's purpose and plan."

Sometimes we get weary in prayer, especially when we don't see a breakthrough and get discouraged when we have a setback that brings a delay to the answer. We become disillusioned when it would be easier to give up than to press on and to press into God. We begin to wonder if what we are praying for will ever come to pass. We must persevere until God says otherwise. The word "persevere" means to remain steadfast, to endure, to stand firm, and not lose courage under pressure.

> There are moments when we must be persistent in prayer even though our emotion within us wants to quit. We may be called upon to be persistent, for a nation, our family, those desperately needing God's touch. God has the victory—He wants our heart and willingness to pray. He will do the rest (Terry Teykl, ***The Presence Based Church***).

Jesus spoke much about the need for perseverance as He said, "Ask, and it will be given to you; seek and you will find; knock, and it will be opened to you. For everyone who asks receives, and he who seeks finds, and to him who knocks it will be opened" (Matthew 7:7-8). Could it be the reason we lose heart and become discouraged about that for which we are praying and does not readily come to pass is we conclude it must not be God's will?

Our conclusion concerning the will of God may not be the case at all. Could it be He wants to know how badly we desire that for which we are praying and not give up in the face of weariness, doubts, and unbelief? Jesus wants us to press into Him and become more focused upon Him than the need for which we are praying (Matthew 6:33).

God has given us His Spirit to help us pray, to empower us to pray, to pray for the mind of the Lord, and to pray from the place of victory (Romans 8:25-26).

Persevering prayer:

- Speaks of the desire in which we pray. It describes our intensity and passion with which we pray.
- Speaks of the determination in our heart to see that for which we are praying come to pass. It describes how relentless we are in our praying.
- Speaks of the desperation we have for God to move and work on our behalf. It describes the great need for breakthrough and victory.
- Speaks of the depth of our commitment to pray until something happens. It describes the declarations and decrees we make and the disposition of the heart that rests in the promises of God.

THE POWER OF SPIRIT-ASSISTED PRAYER

Paul helps us understand the role and the ministry of the Holy Spirit in prayer, "Likewise the Spirit also helps us in our weaknesses. For we do not know what we should pray for as we ought, but the Spirit Himself makes intercession for us with groanings which cannot be uttered" (Romans 8:26). The word "weakness" is not speaking of physical sickness or disease, but the limitation of our humanity to know how to pray with power and authority. The Holy Spirit helps us to know how to pray. He prays for us and through us. In our weakness, we discover the Holy Spirit intercedes for us, and God's grace empowers us to know how to pray.

Diary entries of one man who persevered and overcame:

- Sunday morning May 5: preached in St. Anne's. Asked not to come back.
- Sunday evening: preached in St. John's. Deacons said, "Get out, and stay out."
- Sunday morning May 12: preached in St. Jude's. Can't go back there either.
- Sunday morning May 19: preached in St. Somebody else's. Deacons called a special meeting and said I couldn't return.
- Sunday morning May 26: preached on the street and was kicked off the street.
- Sunday morning June 2: preached at the edge of town and was kicked off the highway.
- Sunday p.m. June 2: preached in a pasture. Ten thousand came.

> These [above] are actual entries from the diaries of John Wesley, one of the greatest revivalists who ever preached. Like Wesley, there are times in your life when it seems like nothing you are doing counts for the kingdom of God and that God isn't listening. Be assured; He is always listening (Cindy Jacobs, ***The Power of Persistent Prayer***).

Paul exhorts us, "and let us not grow weary while doing good, for in due season we shall reap if we do not lose heart" (Galatians 6:9). The temptation to loosen our grip in the midst of the battle is always before us. The pressure to run—to escape—is constant. We are called to persevere amid setbacks, discouraging times, and delays in life. Persevering prayer can do a more profound work in us when we have to press into God for the answer. Persevering prayer can mature us and strengthen us in our walk with Christ. Perseverance is how God transforms our character into the likeness of Christ.

> We look at our newly developed character, which has grown strong through perseverance. God looks at our character, forged in the fire of overcoming delays and battle, and says, "Good, this is what I was waiting for" (Francis Frangipane, ***This Day We Fight***).

Second, through persevering, passionate prayer, we must take prayer to a new level. We must seek new strategies for prayer. Jesus did not pray the same way for everyone. We must receive God's power with which to pray.

Dr. Vincent Synan, noted church historian, tells about the passion of the early Methodist movement:

> Let me summarize: the heritage of the early Methodist was one of fiery camp meetings where people would flock to the altars seeking more of God. The early Methodist was the largest, fastest growing church in the world because of how God moved in the tent revivals. Ironically the world would come to criticize the Methodist for being too noisy! Let me add, that would not be the case today.

They were passionate prayers and worshipers, and there was no mountain too large they could not overcome. Our prayer is: God, do it again. The early Methodists measured their success not by the rewards of growth, but by the faithfulness of God to show up and do marvelous things called signs, wonders, and miracles.

> The vision of the need for which you pray must become a burning passion for seeing God's answer. It must become a deep principle within you that dedicates itself to getting the answer. It must become a compelling drive. It must add fervency to your praying and put the iron of determination within your soul. You must not accept no for an answer (Wesley L. Duewel, ***Mighty Prevailing Prayer***).

Jesus describes the call and ministry of John the Baptist, "And from the days of John the Baptist until now the kingdom of heaven suffers violence, and the violent take it by force" (Matthew 11:1-12). Jesus continues to say, "The Law and the prophets were until John. Since that time the kingdom of God has been preached, and everyone is pressing into it" (Luke 16:16).

Prevailing prayer requires greater power and strength that comes from the kingdom of God to combat apathy, indifference, powerlessness, and lethargy.

Jesus said advancing the kingdom of God is a result of two things: preaching (Good News) and pressing in. Advancing the kingdom involves spiritual passion instead of passivity. To press into God through prayer means to be bold, courageous, and surrender our way for God's way.

> Faith may quietly press in, or it may cry out loudly, but is always violent in the spirit world. It grabs hold of an invisible reality and won't let go. Taking the Kingdom by faith is the violent act that is necessary to come into what God has made available (Bill Johnson, ***When Heaven Invades Earth***).

Persevering prayer is the place where we draw near to God with a pure heart, with a passion for His presence, in the power of the Holy Spirit. We ask that the Spirit of holiness would rest upon us (Romans 1:4) and that He would make Himself known through us by the Spirit of wisdom, and revelation, by the Spirit of counsel and might, and by the Spirit of knowledge and fear of the Lord (Isaiah 11:2).

> It has been my keen awareness of the necessity of the Presence of God in church life that has driven my passion for praying and to "build the church in prayer." The house of prayer is built for the Presence of God to dwell—not visit or look at, but actually, inhabit (Terry Teykl, ***The Presence Based Church***).

Passionate Prayer:

- Originates in the heart, is conveyed to the mind, and spoken through our voice.
- Changes events, history, circumstances, and mobilizes all of heaven to move mountains.
- Prays with conviction, without ceasing, and with confidence. Paul writes, "For the kingdom of God is not in word [the creeds we declare] but in power [that transforms]" (1 Corinthians 4:20).

Third, we release the power of God through persevering invitational prayer. We are inviting the presence and power of God to be in our midst. Jesus is waiting for an invitation to come and make Himself known to us.

> "Something happens when we come to that vulnerable place where we invite Jesus into the places where we're living" (Michael Slaughter, ***Unlearning Church***).

To invite the Lord is to:

- Ask Him to open the eyes of our hearts to see what He is doing (Matthew 13:16; John 9:15; Ephesians 1:18).
- Ask Him to stir up the gifts of the Holy Spirit within us (Deuteronomy 34:9; Isaiah 11:2; 1 Timothy 4:14; 2 Timothy 1:16).
- Ask Him to awaken our hearts to the overwhelming love of God (Romans 13:11-14; 1 Corinthians 15:34).
- Ask Him to let us experience His presence in our lives to a greater degree (Psalm 16:11, 42:2).
- Ask Him to make us a vessel through which His Spirit can flow like a river (John 7:37-39).

GROWTH POINT: Which of these five truths about inviting the Lord are you asking Him to do in you?

> In prevailing prayer, you are asking God to do things you can accomplish in no other way. To prevail you need to desire and hunger deeply, to pray with fervor and passion. In addition, however, you need the dynamic of faith (Wesley L. Duewel, ***Mighty Prevailing Prayer***).

THE POWER OF INVITATION

God uses all who will make themselves available to Him. God looks for anyone who invites the activity of the Holy Spirit to work in and through them. God looks for those who will take Him at His Word, believe it, receive it, and stand upon it until His Word comes to pass in our lives or the lives of others.

Invitational prayer is the lifestyle of trusting the Lord in and for all things. Inviting the Lord to be in our midst is to experience the heart of God.

- It is the place of everlasting joy (Isaiah 35:10).
- It is the place where the power of God keeps us (1 Peter 1:5).
- It is the place of rest (Matthew 11:28).
- It is the place of abiding (John 15:5).

Faith takes the restrictions, the limitations, and the control off of God and invites Him to do the impossible. Jeremiah the Prophet declares, "Ah, Lord God! Behold, You have made the heavens and the earth by Your great power and outstretched arm. There is nothing too hard [difficult] for You" (Jeremiah 32:17).

Let's invite the Lord of all the earth to do something mighty and powerful on our behalf. Let's ask Him into those places that cause difficulty and believe Him for a breakthrough. Let's invite Him into the areas of our lives in which we struggle and believe Him for freedom and healing. Let's ask Him to direct our steps, to fulfill our days with good things and to live in the power of the Holy Spirit.

Hosting the presence of God means to welcome Him, to invite Him, and to make room for Him. Jesus said, "Foxes have holes and birds of the air have nests, but the Son of Man has nowhere to lay His head" (Luke 9:58).

We not only invite Jesus to be in us and to live through us, but He too invites us into vital union with Him.

Prayer is God's invitation to us to work with Him bringing the kingdom of God to be present among us. He invites us to co-labor with Him in the world to be salt, light, and ambassadors for Him. We are commanded to continue the works that He did (John 14:12).

ZACCHAEUS DISCOVERS LIFE IN HIS PRESENCE

Jesus looks for receptive people. "Zacchaeus, make haste and come down, for today I must stay at your house" (Luke 19:5). Jesus wanted to abide, to stay, and to remain at Zacchaeus' home. Jesus was looking for a place to take up residence. He wanted to be in a relationship with him. Jesus wanted Zacchaeus to know Him personally for life is in His presence.

Upon hearing and responding to Christ's invitation to come down so He could stay at his house, Zacchaeus hurriedly came down and received Jesus joyfully. The invitation to Zacchaeus was that Jesus wanted a relationship with him. Zacchaeus heard the life-giving words of Jesus when He said, "Today salvation has come to this house, because he also is a son of Abraham; for the Son of Man has come to seek and to save that which was lost" (Luke 19:9-

10). Zacchaeus received a revelation (understanding) about Jesus he had not known before: Jesus came to find the lost. The understanding of this truth came when Jesus desired to remain with Zacchaeus. Life is in His presence. Transformation takes place in the presence of Jesus.

Prayer releases the power of God to pray with perseverance, to pray with passion, and to invite the Lord to be in our midst. We hear His invitation to come and abide or live with Him. Zacchaeus expressed the unspoken prayer of perseverance until he found a place from which he could see Jesus. He remained there with a heart filled with passion and desire for the touch of Jesus upon his life. He responded to the invitation of Jesus to come down from the tree for He wanted to spend time with him. Zacchaeus' invitation to Jesus was to make Him the Source of his life. "And Zacchaeus stood and said to the Lord, 'Behold, Lord, the half of my goods I give to the poor. And if I have defrauded anyone of anything, I restore it fourfold'" (Luke 19:8, ESV). Persevering prayer releases the power of God to work on our behalf and behalf of others.

PRAY THIS WITH ME

Jesus, we invite You into every area of our lives as you transform us into Your image—Your likeness. Empower us by Your Spirit to pray with perseverance that refuses to give up and with a passion that seeks Your face. You are the desire of our hearts, and nothing satisfies us like You. Take us in our prayer life where we have never been before. Amen!

LET'S TALK ABOUT IT

1. Review the questions in the lesson and discuss your responses.

2. Why is persevering prayer so important?

3. What does it mean that prayer is invitational?

4. How does the Spirit assist us in our praying?

5. What does it mean to pray with passion?

6. How did Zacchaeus express the prayer of perseverance and passionate prayer?

7. How did Zacchaeus respond to Jesus' invitation? How did this invitation change his life?

8. What spoke to you the most from this lesson?

Lesson 6

LISTENING PRAYER

⌘

Listening prayer is taking time to hear the voice of God. We are His sheep, and His sheep hear His voice (John 10:27). Listening prayer is learning to hear the voice of God. For example, Eli, the priest, was instructed to raise Samuel in the temple when Hannah gave birth to Samuel, as a gift from God. One evening Samuel kept hearing voices thinking it was Eli speaking to him. Eli told Samuel when he hears the voice again, say, "Speak, for your servant hears" (1 Samuel 3:10, ESV). We take time to listen to what the Lord is saying intentionally, and we respond to His voice. Communication is two-way: we speak our prayers to the Lord, and we listen to His response. In other words, what goes up will come back down as God pours out His answers upon us.

Learning to hear the voice of God is one of the most important things we can do in developing our prayer life and being followers of Jesus.

ADAM AND EVE

Prayer is more than one-way communication. Prayer is listening intently to the voice of God. The Psalmist says "the voice of the Lord is powerful; the voice of the Lord is full of majesty" (Psalm 29:4). Hearing the voice of God goes back to the garden when Adam and Eve "heard the sound of the Lord God walking in the garden" (Genesis 3:8). Adam said, "I heard Your voice in the garden, and I was afraid because I was naked; and I hid myself" (Genesis 3:10).

Though disobedience had entered into the picture, Adam and Eve still recognized God's voice. Even if we have failed miserably, the Lord still hears our voice, and we can still hear His voice calling us. This gives us hope that when the Lord speaks to us we can hear His voice and respond in obedience.

ELIJAH

Listening prayer is one of the most rewarding activities in our walk with Christ. The Spirit of God awakens us and gives us the ability to hear His voice and the power to walk in obedience. Elijah was at his wit's end and went into a cave to hide. Following a series of events, he heard the still small voice of God speaking to him, giving him instruction what he was to do next (1 Kings 19:11-16). Hearing the voice of God enabled him to fulfill the Lord's assignment and to secure God's future leadership for His people. In our weakest moment, we can hear the voice of God as He instructs us in the way we should go and receive the power of His Spirit to do it.

ISAIAH

In Isaiah chapter six, Isaiah the prophet heard the voice of God that shook the doorposts of the house of God, and the place filled with the glory of God (Isaiah 6:4). He heard the voice of God say, “Whom shall I send, and who will go for us?” Isaiah responded, “Here am I! Send me”(Isaiah 6:8). Hearing the voice of God is the assurance needed to follow His leadership and the empowerment to obey His voice.

Learning to hear the voice of God is the conviction He is still speaking today. He still has something to say to us. We continually look for His voice in all things and every place. We learn to live from His voice. His Words are spirit, and they are life.

JESUS

The way to obedience is to hear God’s voice. We can know what the Lord wants us to do when we hear His voice. Jesus only spoke what He heard the Father say. “I speak to the world those things which I heard from Him” (John 8:26b). Hearing the voice of God is life-giving, for His words are Spirit, and they are life (John 6:68). Jesus said, “Take My yoke upon you and learn from Me” (Matthew 11:29). If we are going to hear the voice of God, then we must learn the way Jesus did as He went about life, ministry, and relationships. Jesus was dependent upon His Father; He only did what He saw the Father doing. To be a follower of Jesus, we must follow Him in His steps and do as He did in hearing the Father’s voice and live from His voice. Life is in the voice.

OBSERVATION: How did hearing the voice of God impact Adam and Eve, Elijah, Isaiah, and Jesus?

HEARING THE VOICE OF GOD

First of all, God is still speaking to us today. If we have determined God has already said all that He is going to say, then we will not take the time to hear what He has to say to us now. "Jesus Christ is the same yesterday, today, and forever" (Hebrews 13:8). We are not talking about adding to Scripture; we are talking about Him having a Word for us that encourages, builds up, and brings comfort. His Word directs our steps and confirms us in the way we should go. His mercies are new every morning, and we need fresh bread from the Lord each day from which to live. Jesus said, "Man shall not live by bread alone, but by every word that proceeds from the mouth of God" (Matthew 4:4). The only conclusion is God still speaks to us today.

Second, God's Word is alive and active. The Father has something to say to us that fills us, equips us, and empowers us. The writer of Hebrews declares, "For the word of God is alive and powerful" (Hebrews 4:12a). His Word touches our lives and imparts life. Jesus speaks words of life that fill, nurture, and empower us to live an overcoming life. His words are actively working for our good and His glory.

Third, God has given us His Spirit to hear His voice. We are God's sons and daughters. We are part of the family of God, and He has given us His Spirit to hear His voice (Romans 8:14-16). Our spirit has been made alive to hear and respond to the voice of God. His Spirit bears witness with our spirit as He leads us into all the truth (John 16:13). God has given us His Spirit so we can hear His voice and walk in obedience.

Fourth, God awakens our understanding to receive His Word. God's Word brings strength, hope, and wisdom. "The Sovereign Lord has given me his words of wisdom so that I know how to comfort the weary. Morning by morning He awakens me and opens my understanding to His will. The Sovereign Lord has spoken to me, and I have listened" (Isaiah 50:4-5a, NLT). What a powerful verse from which to live and to see the Lord as our Source. God speaks to us so we may know His will, purpose, calling, and destiny. He does not want us to be unknowing, but to know and understand His will (Ephesians 5:17).

Fifth, we quiet ourselves before Him. The Psalmist declares, "Be still, and I know that I am God" (Psalm 46:10). Like Samuel, we might even say, "Speak Lord for your servant is listening" (1 Samuel 3:10). It is learning to tune everything out and to turn our face to seek the Lord. It is learning to cultivate the secret place (Matthew 6:4).

> "We close the door to our secret place to shut out all distracting voices and tune our hearts to the one voice which we long to hear" (Bob Sorge, ***Secrets of the Secret Place***).

Quieting ourselves before the Lord is one of the greatest challenges, but it is one of the greatest rewards in the life of the believer. Amongst all the voices that are clamoring for our attention, getting quiet enough to discern His voice is a challenge, but we press into this truth to make it our own.

Quieting ourselves begins with our focus on the Lord, fixing our eyes upon Him. It means to lay aside distractions and make Him the desire and focus of the heart. It is taking time to hear His voice for He has something to say to us.

Sixth, is learning to wait upon the Lord. Isaiah encourages us. "But those who wait on the Lord shall renew their strength; they shall mount up with wings like eagles, they shall run and not be weary, they shall walk and not faint" (Isaiah 40:31). We wait for our expectation is from the Lord (Psalm 62:5). Quieting ourselves and waiting upon the Lord go hand-in-hand. Waiting is the activity of listening with intention, expectation, and faith. When we wait upon the Lord He will speak to us for we are doing what He asks us to do.

- Waiting is one of the most restful, peaceful, and rewarding things we can do.
- Waiting gives time for the Lord to work on our behalf.
- Waiting expresses our desire to know His way.
- Waiting gives time for the Lord to do a deep work in us.

We are not wasting our time when we wait upon the Lord; instead, it propels us into a new dimension of living a fruitful and joyful life. It is here that we are learning to cast all our cares upon the Lord.

GROWTH POINT: Which of the above six ways are you asking God to grow in hearing His voice?

> Things don't change when I talk to God; things change when God talks to me. When I talk, nothing happens; when God talks, the universe comes into existence. So the power of prayer is found, not in convincing God of my agenda, but waiting upon Him to hear His agenda (Bob Sorge, ***Secrets of the Secret Place***).

Listening prayer:

- Is asking God a question, listening to His response, and recording your thoughts. For example: "What does it mean to walk in love and to give it away?" or "How can I be a more forgiving person?"
- Is when we read the Scriptures and record our prayer from that Scripture. For example, we can pray Psalm 16:10: "You will show me the path of life; in your presence is fullness of joy; at Your right hand are pleasures forevermore."
- Is when we say, "Speak Lord, your servant is listening" or by saying, "I am Your sheep, and I hear Your voice" (1 Samuel 3:10; John 10:27), or "Give me ears to hear what the Spirit is saying" (Revelation 3:7, 11, 17, 29).

One of the great ways of testing what we hear is to record our thoughts and find someone with whom you can share those thoughts. You might ask, "Does this sound like God?" The more we practice, the easier it comes, and it brings great joy to the heart. When we hear His voice, we want to obey what He says, and that is the place of blessing and reward. "Blessed are all who hear the Word of God and put it into practice" (Luke 11:28, NLT).

Why must we learn to hear the voice of God?

These are just some of the ways we can begin to practice hearing the voice of God. We cannot depend upon someone else to hear for us; we must learn to hear for ourselves. We may need others to confirm what He is saying. But, we take responsibility to hear God for ourselves concerning His purpose and destiny for our lives, our family, our community, our church, and for the world. The more we grow in hearing God's voice, the more He can share His heart with us.

Every believer can hear the voice of God.

LEARNING TO HEAR THE VOICE OF GOD

Four keys to hearing the voice of God by Mark Virkler:

1. God's voice in your heart often sounds like a flow of spontaneous thoughts (Habakkuk 2:2).
2. Become still so you can sense God's flow of thoughts and emotions (Psalm 46:10).
3. As you pray, fix the eyes of your heart upon Jesus (Habakkuk 2:1-2; Hebrews 12:2).
4. Journal the thoughts, prayers, and impressions that you receive from the Lord (Habakkuk 2:2, Ephesians 1:18).

EXERCISE IN HEARING GOD'S VOICE

Use Psalm 1 in this exercise. First of all, read through the passage of Scripture below. Don't try to analyze your thoughts, but let them flow like a river full of life. Next, record what you are hearing. For example, some may have a picture. Begin recording what you see. Some may have a verse(s) of Scripture that comes to you. Record what you hear.

There is not a right or wrong way of doing this, for we are learning to hear God's voice and recording what we hear. Take a few minutes to do this exercise. Read Psalm 1 and record your thoughts as to what you sense the Lord is saying to you.

> Blessed is the man who walks not in the counsel of the ungodly, nor stands in the path of sinners, nor sits in the seat of the scornful; But his delight is in the law of the Lord, and in His law he meditates day and night. He shall be like a tree planted by the rivers of water, that brings forth its fruit in its season, whose leaf also shall not wither; and whatever he does shall prosper. The ungodly are not so, but are like the chaff which the wind drives away. Therefore the ungodly shall not stand in the judgment, nor sinners in the congregation of the righteous. For the Lord knows the way of the righteous, but the way of the ungodly shall perish (Psalm 1).

Record your thoughts:

PRAY THIS WITH ME

Father, You lead us in all the right ways that lead to abundant life. Father, help us to hear Your voice in all places and at all times. Help us to be intentional about hearing Your voice so that we may walk in obedience. You lead us in the paths of righteousness. We are Your sheep, and we desire to hear Your voice and to be led by Your Spirit. Give us ears to hear what the Spirit is saying. Amen!

LET'S TALK ABOUT IT

1. Review the questions in the lesson and discuss your responses.

2. How and in what way does God speak to us? Why must we be open to hearing from God in different ways?

3. What does it mean that every believer can hear the voice of God? Why are we able to hear His voice?

Fill in the Blank with these answer choices:

speaking, awakens, wait, Spirit, childlike, important, Word, quiet

A. We believe that God is still ____________ to us today.
B. We come to the Lord in ________________ faith.
C. We believe that God's _______________ is alive and active.
D. God _______________ our hearing to understand His will.
E. Hearing the voice of God is learning to __________ upon the Lord.
F. Hearing the voice of God, we ____________ ourselves before the Lord.
G. Learning to hear the voice of God is one of the most ______________ things we can do in developing our prayer life.

4. What are you asking the Father to do as a result of this lesson?

Lesson 7

Praying the Word

⌘

> My first discovery was that people in every place and at every time have "prayed the Bible." It was shocking to find that for thousands of years, men and women of God have used the model of praying the Bible—out loud—every day! (Wesley Campbell, ***Welcoming a Visitation of the Holy Spirit***).

WHAT IS PRAYER?

Prayer is a supernatural vehicle created by God allowing human beings to communicate with Him in the supernatural realm. God's plan for us is praying to bring the results of God to earth. That is, whatever is happening in heaven to become a present reality upon the earth, "Your Kingdom come. Your will be done on earth as it is in heaven" (Matthew 6:10). Praying out loud helps us to pray more effectively. God spoke, and the world was created (Genesis 1). The phrase "God said..." occurs ten times in Chapter one of Genesis as a means of bringing life and order. Paul declares faith comes by hearing and hearing the Word of God (Romans 10:17).

When we pray the Word out loud, we hear it, and it builds up our faith. We encourage ourselves as we speak and declare His Word over people, places, and events.

Ezekiel was commanded by God to speak to the dry bones. God said, "Prophesy to these bones, and say to them, 'O dry bones, hear the word of the Lord'" (Ezekiel 37:4). God tells us to speak to the mountain, "I say to you, if you have faith as a mustard seed, you will say to this mountain, 'Move from here to there,' and it will move; and nothing will be impossible for you" (Matthew 17:20). Prayer is speaking to those things that stand in our way from living a victorious overcoming life and telling them they must go.

There is something powerful released when we use the Word of God to speak to the mountains in our lives. When we pray the Bible, everything comes into submission to His Word. We read the Word, we study the Word, we hear the Word, but the Bible says we can speak the Word. Jesus said the words He spoke to us are spirit, and they are life (John 6:63). When we speak—declare out loud—we are declaring words of life where there is death. We speak words of encouragement where there is discouragement. We speak words of victory over defeat. To pray the Word, breaks down barriers and builds bridges.

THE POWER SOURCE OF PRAYER

When the Word of God is applied to our situations and dilemmas, we are applying the Holy Spirit and life. Jesus said, "The words that I speak to you are spirit, and they are life" (John 6:63b). When applying God's Word to our challenges, our struggles, and our problems, we allow the Word of God to speak to that situation. We take hold of the promises of God and apply His promises to our problems.

When we apply the Word of God, we are taking the words of the Bible off the pages, and applying them directly to life situations, to our problems, and to everything that would keep us from living an overcoming life in Christ.

> This really gives prayer its power, that I take God's thoughts from His Word, and present them before Him. Then I am enabled to pray according to God's Word. How indispensable God's Word is for all true prayer! (Andrew Murray, ***God's Best Secrets***).

Paul writes, "So then faith comes by hearing, and hearing by the word of God" (Romans 10:17). When we pray out loud, we are hearing the Word, and our faith comes alive. We are built up and encouraged by the Word of God as we speak it out loud. There is something revolutionary and transformational that takes place when we begin to stand on the Bible to declare His Word to come to pass. Jesus said, "If you abide in Me, and My words abide in you, you will ask what you desire, and it shall be done for you" (John 15:7). May the Words of Jesus so resonate in our spirit that we will know how to pray.

When God's Word abides in us, they bring healing to the sick, freedom to the captive, and comfort to the afflicted. When we pray the Word of God, we give ourselves a faith lift.

We can pray His will with confidence and expectation when we pray His Word. The will of God is found in His Word, and it helps us to navigate through life's ups and downs and to live from God's perspective. When we know what He has said in His Word, we can pray with boldness.

The key to understanding His Word is to hide it in our hearts (Psalm 119:11).

When we hide His Word in our hearts, it gives us greater confidence with which to pray. Jude observes that we are to "build each other up in your most holy faith, pray in the power of the Holy Spirit" (Jude 20, NLT).

I understand this to be our prayer language as we pray in the power of the Holy Spirit, or Spirit-inspired prayers that move us, build us up, and release us to do mighty ministry in the name of Jesus. The Holy Spirit breathed upon the Word of God and inspired it, "All Scripture is God-breathed [given by divine inspiration]" (2 Timothy 3:16a, AMP). When we pray the Word, we are praying in the power of the Holy Spirit. We are praying Spirit-inspired prayers that do the mighty works of God.

> "Using the Word in prayer is not taking it out of context, for His Word in us is the key to answered prayer—the prayer that brings results" (Germaine Copeland, ***Prayers That Avail Much***).

FROM THE NATURAL TO THE SUPERNATURAL

To pray powerfully is to know there is nothing too hard for God (Jeremiah 32:17b). When praying the Word of God, we go from the seen to the unseen, from the limited to the unlimited, and from our ability to His ability" who is able to do exceedingly abundantly above all that we ask or think, according to the power that works in us" (Ephesians 3:20).

"The power lies within God's Word. It is anointed by the Holy Spirit. The Spirit of God does not lead us apart from the Word, for the Word is of the Spirit of God" (Germaine Copeland, ***Prayers That Avail Much***).

WE BEGIN TO DESIRE WHAT HE DESIRES

Praying the Word of God enables us to see things from His perspective, from His viewpoint. When we pray the Word of God, we receive His mind (understanding, insight, wisdom) in knowing how to pray in a way that brings glory to God.

What makes praying the Word of God so powerful?

"Praying the Word is the most powerful weapon we have in our prayer arsenal" (Cindy Jacobs, ***The Power of Persistent Prayer***).

PRAYER DECLARATIONS AND PRAYER APPLICATIONS

When we pray scriptural prayers back to the Lord, we declare His goodness and greatness. Try speaking this prayer from Psalm 63 out loud to the Lord. It may be awkward at first because we hear ourselves pray aloud or read the Bible out loud. Keep practicing, and it will be easier and become a wonderful blessing to you.

> O God, you are my God; I earnestly search for you. My soul thirsts for you; my whole body longs for you in this parched and weary land where there is no water. I have seen you in your sanctuary and gazed

> upon your power and glory. Your unfailing love is better than life itself; how I praise you! I will praise you as long as I live, lifting up my hands to you in prayer. You satisfy me more than the richest feast. I will praise you with songs of joy (Psalm 63:1-5, NLT).

Begin to pray this back to the Father, speaking of your heart's desire for more of Him and how you look for Him in the sanctuary to see His power and His glory. Declare that His love is unfailing as you lift your hands to the Lord in surrender and worship. Our heavenly Father desires to satisfy the deepest longings of the heart. Spend time repeating this Psalm back to the Lord until it becomes your prayer.

Let me illustrate praying the Scriptures with my prayer:

> *Father, You are my God, and I seek You with my whole heart. My heart thirsts for You and You satisfy the deepest longings of my heart. Father, I come seeking Your presence among Your people lifting my hands and my life as an offering of praise and thanksgiving to You. Father, I surrender myself to Your highest will and purpose. Amen!*

Record your prayer from Psalm 63:1-5

Author and speaker Bob Sorge gives four reasons for praying the Scriptures:

> First of all, we discover the nature of prayer and its importance to the purpose and plan of God for our lives (John 17:20-21). Second, it animates our praying because God's Word is the expression of His will (Ps. 40:8). Third, it strengthens our prayer because the Word we pray is often God's power demonstrated through our prayers (Heb. 4:12; Is. 55:11). Fourth, we are praying prayers that express God's feelings and emotions (Jer. 31:32) (Bob Sorge, ***Secrets of the Secret Place***).

We are learning to pray God's Word using personal pronouns. Praying God's Word by making it personal—your own—is a powerful way to pray.

Scripture (read this aloud):

> The righteous shall flourish like a palm tree, he shall grow like a cedar in Lebanon. Those who are planted in the house of the Lord shall flourish in the courts of our God. They shall still bear fruit in old age; they shall be fresh and flourishing, to declare that the Lord is upright; He is my rock, and there is no unrighteousness in Him (Psalm 92:12-15).

Let me illustrate with my prayer:

> *I am the righteousness of God in Christ Jesus, and I shall flourish like a palm tree. I shall grow like a cedar in Lebanon, and the roots of my life will grow deep in the soil of God's love. The Lord plants me in His house, and*

I shall flourish in the courts of my God like a well-watered garden. I shall bear fruit in my old age; I shall be fresh and thriving in the gifts and callings of God. I will declare that the Lord is upright, good, and just. He is my rock, and I stand forever in God's righteousness. Amen!

When we pray the Word:

- We pray with authority for God's Word carries authority (2 Timothy 3:16-17).
- We pray the truth for God's Word is truth (John 17:17).
- We pray the will of God to be done on earth as it is in heaven (Matthew. 6:10).
- We are abiding in Him for we are His disciples (John 15:7-8).
- We release God's life-giving Word (John 6:63, 68).
- We pray with purity for every Word of God is pure (Proverbs 30:5).
- We pray the creative Word of God for life is in the voice (Genesis 1:1-3; Ezekiel 37:1-10).

GROWTH POINT: Which of the above seven ways of praying the Word are you asking God to help you grow?

To pray the Word is:

1. Deciding to apply God's Word to our daily lives. We live from every word that proceeds from the mouth of God.
2. Declaring God's Word to be true as we stand on His promises to come to pass in our lives.

3. Decreeing God's Word to act on our behalf. We rest in the confidence that God is always working to fulfill His Word. "For I am [actively] watching over My word to fulfill it" (Jeremiah 1:12b, AMP).

Write out your prayer below making it personal and using your declaration about God and yourself using Psalm 92:12-15.

Record your prayer below:

IN SUMMARY

- Prayer is a carrier God uses to bring His will to earth.
- Prayer loaded with God's Word sees answers to our prayers.
- Prayer was created for God's purpose to communicate with His sons and daughters.
- Prayer is joining in agreement with God to execute His will and desires; it will prevail over the enemy who comes only to steal, kill, and destroy. God's power is released by agreeing with His Word in prayer.

Let me suggest taking the next several weeks and pray these apostolic (prayers Paul prayed for the churches he served) prayers found in Ephesians 1:15-23; Philippians 1:3-11; Colossians 1:9-14. I suggest that you personalize the prayer by inserting the personal pronouns "I," "me," or "mine." You may also want to insert the names of your family and begin praying these prayers over your family. You might want to pray these prayers over your church by inserting the name of your church. Let me suggest you write out your prayers as you learn to pray the Word and pray it out loud.

LET'S TALK ABOUT IT

1. Review the questions in the lesson and discuss your responses.

2. What does it mean to pray the Word?

3. How can praying the Word change our lives?

4. What happens when we pray the Word?

5. What happens when we apply the Word of God to our situation?

6. What does it mean when we pray the Word we are praying God's life-giving Word.

7. How do you think praying God's Word can impact our daily lives?

8. What are you asking the Father to do as a result of this lesson?

Lesson 8

WIND, FIRE, AND LANGUAGE

⌘

> When the Day of Pentecost had fully come, they [the disciples of Jesus] were all with one accord in one place. And suddenly there came a sound from heaven, as of a mighty rushing wind, and it filled the whole house where they were sitting. Then there appeared to them divided tongues, as of fire, and sat upon each of them. And they were all filled with the Holy Spirit and began to speak in other tongues, as the Spirit gave them utterance. And there were dwelling in Jerusalem Jews, devout men, from every nation under heaven. And when this sound occurred, the multitude came together, and were confused, because everyone heard them speak in his own language (Acts 2:1-6).

BREAKTHROUGH PRAYER

The disciples had been praying, agreeing together that what Jesus said would come to pass; they would receive the gift of the Father, the Holy Spirit. Through committed prayer and great anticipation of what was yet to come, they believed the words of Jesus and obeyed His command to wait in Jerusalem to receive the gift of the Holy Spirit. When their breakthrough came, it caused a great commotion. It generated curiosity and caused the hearts of men to inquire what was this all about and how they should respond (Acts 2:37-39).

The messages of John the Baptist and Jesus did not stop at just repentance.

John the Baptist states, "I indeed baptize you with water unto repentance, but He who is coming after me is mightier than I, whose sandals I am not worthy to carry. He will **baptize you with the Holy Spirit and fire**" (Matthew 3:11, emphasis added).

Jesus told the disciples they would declare the Good News of the Gospel. Peter's first sermon at Pentecost did not end at repentance.

> "And that repentance and remission of sins should be preached in His name to all nations, beginning at Jerusalem. And you are witnesses of these things. Behold, I send the Promise of My Father upon you; but tarry in the city of Jerusalem until you are endued with power from on high" (Luke 24:47-49).

Repentance points to a greater encounter, the fullness of the Spirit.

> Now when they heard this, they were cut to the heart, and said to Peter and the rest of the apostles, "Men and brethren, what shall we do?" Then Peter said to them, "Repent, and let every one of you be baptized in the name of Jesus Christ for the remission [forgiveness] of sins; and you shall receive the gift of the Holy Spirit" (Acts 2:37-38).

God delights when we seek Him out—"my soul thirsts for You; my flesh longs for You in a dry and thirsty land where there is no water" (Psalm 63:1b). Peter's message provoked their hearts that created a hunger for more. They wanted to have what these disciples were experiencing—an outpouring of the Spirit.

Jesus said, "If you then, being evil, know how to give good gifts to your children, how much more will your heavenly Father give the Holy Spirit to those who ask [and continue to ask] Him!" (Luke 11:13). God delights when we hunger for Him. "Blessed are those who hunger and thirst for righteousness, for they shall be satisfied" (Matthew 5:6, ESV). The NKJV translates this passage as "for they shall be filled" which means to be satisfied with abundance.

> From the very beginning, Jesus made it clear that the principal need of the human race and the only solution to mankind's dilemma was the Kingdom of heaven. "Blessed are the poor in spirit, for theirs is the kingdom of heaven" (Matthew 5:3). In other words, if you are spiritually poor, only the Kingdom will satisfy and fulfill your hunger (Myles Munroe, ***Understanding Your Place in God's Kingdom***).

God delights when we are obedient to His Word that transforms us, empowers us, and equips us for kingdom purposes.

Jesus came preaching the gospel concerning the rule and reign of God evidenced through repentance and empowerment of the Holy Spirit. We draw upon the obedience of Christ to live a life obedient to the Father. We love because the Holy Spirit has poured God's love into our hearts. We cherish and nurture the life of Christ as He expresses Himself through us.

POWERPOINT: The disciples witnessed the flames of fire resting on their heads; they released a language that glorified God and witnessed to His love as the Spirit poured into their hearts. Those who were present testified to this event as they heard the message of Jesus in their language. Pentecost was the invasion of God upon the human heart transformed by the power of the Holy Spirit.

The wind would blow away their fears, the fire of the Spirit would be ablaze in their hearts, and the language of the Spirit would fill their mouths with the Good News of Jesus.

EXAMINING THE EVIDENCE

First of all, the disciples were filled with the wind, the breath of God (Acts 2:2). Jesus described to Nicodemus concerning the work of the Holy Spirit, "The wind blows where it wishes, and you hear the sound of it, but cannot tell where it comes from and where it goes. So is everyone who is born of the Spirit" (John 3:8).

The wind of the Spirit blows upon the face of the earth as in the case of Noah, "Then God remembered Noah, and every living thing, and all the animals that were with him in the ark. And God made a wind to pass over the earth, and the waters subsided" (Genesis 8:1). To the hungry Israelites wandering in the wilderness, God provided the wind of the Spirit that would blow provision for the children of Israel,

"Now a wind went out from the Lord, and it brought quail from the sea" (Numbers 11:31a).

Wind is a manifestation of the Holy Spirit's presence as He fills the vacuum of the human heart.

Let us release the Spirit of God through prayer, intercession, and worship. Jesus said, "The words that I speak to you are Spirit; and they are life" (John 6:63b). Ezekiel experienced the releasing of God's life-giving Spirit, and we too speak life to dead bones of religiosity, apathy, and spiritual dryness, as God would raise up a mighty army from the dead (Ezekiel 37:1-10).

Let us release the breath, the wind of God's life-giving Words to those areas in our lives that have left us empty and depleted needing the touch of Christ. Let us release the life-giving Words of Jesus to those areas in our lives that have been suppressed by fear, discouragement, and defeat to experience Christ's healing and wholeness. The wind of the Spirit has filled our spirits and has made us alive unto God to release the sounds of heaven, and with the breath of God, we speak life.

Second, the disciples became like burning bushes as tongues of fire rested on their heads (Acts 2:3). The purpose of the Spirit is to make us pure and holy as He burns away things that keep us from giving ourselves entirely to Christ.

The Spirit's purpose is to fuel us with the power to do the mighty works of God with signs, wonders, and miracles.

What does fire do?

- Fire lights up our lives and disperses the darkness.
- Fire is contagious and can be caught by others because of the presence of Jesus in us.
- Fire is what we gather around for its warmth, its light, and its comfort. It unifies the people of God.
- Fire cleanses and purifies.
- Fire is the character quality of God "for our God is a consuming fire" (Hebrews 12:29, ESV).

Remember the words of John the Baptist, "I indeed baptize you with water unto repentance, but He who is coming after me is mightier than I, whose sandals I am not worthy to carry. He will baptize you with the Holy Spirit and fire" (Matthew 3:11).

Father, release a fresh wind of Your Spirit that renews our minds, that inspires our imaginations, and that fills the earth with Your glory (Habakkuk 2:14).

Third, the disciples were able to articulate the message of God's Good News to all peoples (Acts 2:4-11). The disciples were not drunk, but simply overcome with the joy of the Lord and the Spirit's power (Acts 2:14-15). They were experiencing what the Prophet Joel said would happen, "And it shall come to pass in the last days, says God, that I will pour out of My Spirit on all flesh; your sons and daughters shall prophesy, your young men shall see visions, your old men shall dream dreams" (Acts 2:17).

The language that would divide us (Genesis 11:6-9) would now be a language that would unite us with the message of

Jesus Christ, His death on the cross, His resurrection, and His life-giving Spirit. Our forgiveness of sins and the right to sit with Christ in heavenly places became the message of the early followers of Jesus, and the message hasn't changed. All people would now hear the Word of Christ in their language through the Spirit that would supersede everything that would divide us. The language of the Spirit does not separate us, but unites us through the love of Christ poured into our hearts (Romans 5:5).

I realize that many books and commentaries have sought to explain spiritual language or speaking in tongues. I am not trying to add to or to take away from what many have written about this gift. My point is we are talking about prayer and various kinds of prayers. We cannot exclude this subject just because we don't fully understand its function, practice, and role in the church and our lives. We cannot sweep under the rug or cut out some portion of Scripture just because we don't understand it or even believe in it. My point is all the gifts of God are good; they build us up and encourage us. We do not use the gifts of God to divide, but to unite. Love is the motivating factor in the use of all spiritual gifts.

Let me say: Every believer has the opportunity to enjoy a devotional prayer language that builds our faith; it ushers in the presence of God, and empowers us for victorious Christian living.

The language of the Spirit:

- The language of the Spirit communicates the heart of God to His people (Isaiah 28:11-12).

- The language of the Spirit assists us to pray the will, purpose, and plan of God for His people (1 Corinthians 8:26-27).
- The language of the Spirit builds up, encourages, and inspires us (Jude 20).
- The language of the Spirit helps us to understand the mysteries of God (1 Corinthians 14:13-15).
- The language of the Spirit is God's language of love to His sons and daughters (1 Corinthians 13:1).
- The language of the Spirit is the language of worship (Acts 10:44-46).
- The language of the Spirit renews our mind and refreshes our spirit.
- The language of the Spirit releases the gifts of the Spirit and cultivates the fruit of the Spirit.
- The language of the Spirit goes unhindered or uncensored by the enemy, the devil.
- The language of the Spirit creates our hunger for more of the Lord and for the Lord to have more of us.

GROWTH POINT: From the above language of the Spirit, in what way are you asking God to grow?

Let us avail ourselves to the Spirit's language so that we may communicate with the Father in one Spirit, "But he who is joined to the Lord is one spirit with Him" (1 Corinthians 6:17). The language of the Spirit gives us insights needed to pray powerfully with conviction, purpose, and hope. There is hidden power in developing and cultivating our spiritual language. It changes the atmosphere from defeat to victory, from darkness to light, and propels us into our destiny, purpose, and calling.

THE SPIRIT COMES WITH POWER

To make us bold witnesses to the resurrection of Jesus Christ. Peter states, "Men and brethren, let me speak freely [boldly—let me tell it all]... this Jesus God has raised up, of which we are all witnesses" (Acts 2:29a, 32).

Luke writes, "Repentance and remission of sins should be preached in His name to all nations, beginning at Jerusalem. And you are witnesses of these things" (Luke 24:47-48). The resurrection of Jesus from the dead was the keynote message of the early church. They witnessed the fulfillment of Scripture. They witnessed the power to live an overcoming life. They testified to the forgiveness of sins, healing, and wholeness that comes through the person of Jesus Christ.

The Spirit comes filling us with His empowering grace to do in us and through us what we could never do on our own. "And having received from the Father the promise of the Holy Spirit, He poured out this which you now see and hear" (Acts 2:33b).

Paul writes concerning the sufficiency of the grace of God, "My grace is sufficient for you, for My strength is made perfect in weakness. Therefore most gladly I will rather boast of my infirmities, that the power of Christ may rest upon me" (2 Corinthians 12:9). God's empowering grace takes us beyond our weakness and exchanges our weakness for His strength. Paul declares, "Now all glory to God, who is able, through his mighty power at work within us, to accomplish infinitely more than we might ask or think" (Ephesians 3:20, NLT).

God's uses imperfect vessels to bring forth a message of healing, deliverance, and freedom through the empowerment of the Holy Spirit.

God uses us not because of our greatness, or our accomplishments, or our pedigree, or our giftedness, but just because He has chosen "jars of clay" (1 Corinthians 6:19) that are fragile, imperfect, and weak to demonstrate His power and glory.

After the disciples were filled with the Holy Spirit, they discovered:

- A purpose—to be agents of God's love.
- A mission—to be ambassadors for Christ.
- A message—"This is the message which we have heard from Him and declare to you, that God is light and in Him is no darkness at all" (1 John 1:5). The message is filled with the fullness of God as we continue the ministry of Jesus through the empowerment of the Holy Spirit.

PRAY THIS WITH ME

Father, let the fire of Your Spirit fall upon us, consume us, and ignite us with Your love that fills our hearts. Set us ablaze with Your Spirit that changes the landscape of the world around us and impacts the atmosphere of the communities in which we live. Father, empower us to co-labor with You bringing Your Kingdom to be a present reality. Let the wind of Your Spirit blow mightily upon us filling our lungs with Your life-giving Spirit. Let Your language of love arise from within so that we share the message of Jesus Christ—to the least, last, and the lost.

Father, You use jars of clay, just like us, to show forth Your power and glory. Awaken in us to see Your highest will and purpose done and the courage to stand upon Your Word. Father, make us vessels that honor Your name, Your work, Your creation, and Your glory. Amen!

LET'S TALK ABOUT IT

1. Review the questions in the lesson and discuss your responses.

2. What do wind, fire, and language represent in the believer's life?

3. What difference do you think spiritual language could make in our lives?

4. What is the difference between Genesis 11:6-9 the Tower of Babel and Acts 2:11 where the people heard the wonderful works of God in their languages?

5. Describe in your own words what it means when the Spirit comes with power.

6. What one thing are you asking the Father to do as a result of this lesson?

Lesson 9

Prayer—The Place Where God Meets Us

⌘

In Luke chapter 5:1-11, we find a story of four fishermen who have been fishing all night, and they have come up empty. The next morning as they cleaned their nets Jesus asked to use one of the boats from which to preach, for a large group of people had gathered around Him. Peter was glad to lend Him his boat as He spoke to the people.

Jesus finished His message and said to the fishermen, "Launch out into the deep and let down your nets for a catch" (Luke 5:4). This was no small request for it meant getting their boats ready to go back out to sea with no promise of a getting a catch. With great reluctance, they prepared to do as Jesus had asked. This was going to be a place where obedience would produce a great mass of fish that would bring these fishermen to their knees. They would leave everything to launch out to follow Jesus as His disciples. Let's look at these truths more closely.

We find complete trust in Jesus' word was required. Peter said to Jesus, "Master, we have toiled all night and caught nothing; nevertheless at your **word** I will let down the net" (Luke 5:5, emphasis added). Peter and his friends did not have a history with Jesus. He was a stranger to them, but something rose up within them and made them want to obey Jesus' command. The disciples probably said among themselves, "*What do we have to lose? Let's prove to this Man we know how and when to fish better than He does.*" This is obedience—taking Jesus at His Word and watching to see what He will do.

Obedience is called agreement: agreeing with God as to what He wants to do. The opposite is resistance.

Launching out into the deep required:

- A response to **obey**—"Nevertheless at your word…"
- A demonstration of **faith**—"I will let down the net."
- A **teachable spirit**—"When Simon Peter saw it, he fell down at Jesus's knees, saying, Depart from me, for I am a sinful man, O Lord."

> Wherever we are spiritually, God's call is for us to move onward. Choose your own metaphor—higher ground, a closer walk, another step—it is the call of God by the Holy Spirit to greater growth and maturity through **obedience** and faith. The command to launch out into the deep is simply the insistence of the Lord that we go on with Him (Mark Rutland, ***Launch Out Into the Deep***).

Obedience is a willingness to follow God's leadership when we don't understand what it means or being led to do something we have never done before. We simply obey God because we want to please Him in all things, and we have a deep reverence for Him.

What did obedience mean to Peter and his fishing partners?

Peter obeyed the Lord as he launched out into the deep by letting down his nets to catch fish. This act of obedience would lead to other times where obedience would be required. He was once again called on to exercise obedience. It was another opportunity to launch out into the deep and see what God would do.

Let's look at what took place as God poured out His Spirit on all mankind as recorded in Acts 10 and 11. What opened the door for the gift of the Holy Spirit to be poured out upon the Gentiles? In church history, there is strong evidence that prayer precedes revival. Revival happens when men and woman give themselves to pray until God does something.

Prayer changes our attitudes, it affects the spiritual climate around us, and it touches the audience God has given to us.

Peter's encounter with God is one he had never experienced before. It would be a strong message from the Lord that at first was difficult to interpret. On the surface, it looked more like a nightmare for a Jewish person, but beyond the obvious, God was speaking a profound word to Peter that the gospel is for everyone, even to the Gentiles.

Peter was taking a nap before dinner and had a vision of God's plan to reach the nations, though at the moment he was unsure what the vision meant. God uses every means possible to speak to us; and therefore, we must be open to the different ways in which He may speak.

This event began earlier with a man named Cornelius who was devoted to God, had a reverence for Him, was generous in his giving, and had a vital prayer life. (Acts 10:1-2). Obedience began with a vision one afternoon when Cornelius was instructed by an angel to get Peter and gave him instructions where to find him.

> One afternoon about three o'clock, he had a vision in which he saw an angel of God coming toward him. "Cornelius!" the angel said. Cornelius stared at him in terror. "What is it, sir?" he asked the angel. And the angel replied, "Your prayers and gifts to the poor have been received by God as an offering! Now send some men to Joppa, and summon a man named Simon Peter. He is staying with Simon, a tanner who lives near the seashore (Acts 10:3-6, NLT).

Then around noon, Peter had a vision of a sheet coming down from heaven full of animals that were forbidden for Jews to eat. When it was over, Peter wondered what it meant. The men sent by Cornelius arrived at the place where Peter was staying. "While Peter thought about the vision, the Spirit said to him, 'Behold, three men are seeking you. Arise therefore, go down and go with them, doubting nothing; for I have sent them'" (Acts 10:19-20). The phrase "doubting nothing" means don't hesitate, don't have misgivings, don't be double-minded nor waver between hope and fear.

When Peter arrived at Cornelius' home, he told him about his encounter with the Lord though he did not know what the vision meant, "then the Spirit told me go with them, doubting nothing" (Acts 11:12). Jesus said the work of the

Holy Spirit would lead believers into all the truth, "When He, the Spirit of truth, has come, He will guide you into all truth" (John 16:13). As believers, we can expect the Spirit's leadership to be supernatural. Living a supernatural lifestyle means to obey the Word of the Lord, and see what He will do. Later on, when Peter stood before the Jerusalem Council, he gave an account of how God poured out His Spirit on the Gentiles.

> Men and brethren, you know that a good while ago God chose among us, that by my mouth the Gentiles should hear the word of the gospel and believe. So God, who knows the heart, acknowledged them [bore witness] by giving them the Holy Spirit, just as He did to us, and made no distinction between us, and them, purifying their hearts by faith (Acts 15:7-9).

Obedience for Peter:

- Took him beyond his comfort zone, but led to great blessing.
- Gave him the ability to be led by the Spirit into new adventures, new places, and new experiences of ministry.
- Opened the door of salvation and the outpouring of the Holy Spirit for Cornelius, his family, the Gentile community, and eventually to the world.
- Confirmed the mighty work of God to hungry people to know more about the Lord and His love for them.

What did obedience mean to Peter?
What does it mean to us?

WHAT DOES OBEDIENCE MEAN?

First of all, obedience is responding in a childlike way to the Spirit's prompting. It is trusting God when you do not have the complete picture of what He is doing. The servants said to Peter, "Cornelius…was divinely instructed by a holy angel to summon you to his house and to hear words from you" (Acts 10:22). God had been preparing Peter for such an event as this in that he agreed to go (Acts 10:23). Obedience flows out of relationship to Jesus as we hear His voice and are moved to follow the leading of His Spirit (John 10:27). Peter illustrates our need to hear God's voice and to walk in obedience.

Peter arrived at the home of Cornelius, along with some of his close friends. Cornelius began sharing the encounter he had with the angel that happened four days earlier as he was instructed to invite Peter to his home. Cornelius explains, "So I sent to you immediately, and now you have done well to come. Now therefore, we are all present before God, to hear all the things commanded you by God" (Acts 10:33).

OBSERVATION: What does it mean to cooperate with God? What results when we cooperate with Him?

Peter told those who were present about Jesus and "how God anointed Jesus of Nazareth with the Holy Spirit and with power, who went about doing good and healing all who were oppressed by the devil, for God was with Him" (Acts 10:38). God will give us a word in season that speaks to what He is doing at that time. The unveiling of God's message to Cornelius was about to make history. We can live from God's Word because His Word is life-giving (John 6:63).

When asked to speak about our faith, "always be ready to give a defense to everyone who asks you a reason for the hope that is in you, with meekness and fear" (1 Peter 3:15b). This same good news is ours today for Jesus is still "doing good and healing all who are oppressed by the devil" (Acts 10:38b). The writer of Hebrews declares, "Jesus Christ is the same yesterday, today, and forever" (Hebrews 13:8). This lifestyle of obedience comes as a revelation—an unveiling of the heart of the Father. It is a way of life that encompasses surrender and dependence upon the Lord.

Second, obedience comes from our devotional and prayer life. God wants us to be successful in following Him. It will witness to our spirit, and it will be confirmed by others what He is doing. He will put you in the right place, at the right time, with the right people, and it is not by accident. What Peter preached to Cornelius came from Peter's devotional and prayer life. Peter's message below is the fruit of a life devoted to the Lord and to prayer. When we are asked about our faith, our response flows from the intimate relationship that we enjoy with Father. We may not know what to say at the time, but as we open our mouth God will fill it with good things. God's message will speak to the heart of the people and will bring about transformation and the pouring out of God's Spirit.

> You yourselves know what happened throughout all Judea, beginning from Galilee after the baptism that John proclaimed: how God anointed Jesus of Nazareth with the Holy Spirit and with power. He

> went about doing good and healing all who were oppressed by the devil, for God was with him. And we are witnesses of all that he did both in the country of the Jews and in Jerusalem. They put him to death by hanging him on a tree, but God raised him on the third day and made him to appear, not to all the people but to us who had been chosen by God as witnesses, who ate and drank with him after he rose from the dead. And he commanded us to preach to the people and to testify that he is the one appointed by God to be judge of the living and the dead. To him all the prophets bear witness that everyone who believes in him receives forgiveness of sins through his name (Acts 10:37-43, ESV).

These words set Cornelius and his household ablaze with the Spirit. These words filled with the testimony of Peter are life-giving. These words brought about a revelation of the Father's heart. These are the words that would impact an entire culture.

Third, God opened doors that were previously closed. God's Spirit is not for a certain few or a specific group; He pours out His Spirit on all people. "While Peter was still speaking these words, the Holy Spirit fell upon all those who heard the word...because the gift of the Holy Spirit had been poured out on the Gentles also" (Acts 10:44, 45). The fullness of the Holy Spirit flows out of a relationship. Therefore, the normal Christian life is: signs, wonders, and miracles.

Here are truths we live by:

- Through our prayer and devotional life, we can respond to the spontaneous prompting and leading of the Holy Spirit.
- The Holy Spirit leads us to the right people, at the right place, at the right time, and it is not a coincidence. Our prayer life flows from alignment with Jesus so He can give us His assignment to live a supernatural lifestyle.
- God opens doors that in the natural seem impossible, but with God all things are possible. We wait upon the Lord to open all the right doors, we can rest in the assurance that He will lead us in a way that brings glory to His name, and the kingdom of God becomes a present reality.
- We carry the Good News of the Gospel in our hearts and upon our lips. It impacts the world around us. Encounters with Jesus always lead to transformed lives, beginning with our transformation.

Living a supernatural lifestyle is expecting God to do extraordinary things as He lives His life through us. We have God's divine nature living in us (2 Peter 1:4) so that we can live a supernatural lifestyle. The supernatural lifestyle is the fruit of a life devoted to prayer

POWERPOINT: Peter obeyed the prompting of the Holy Spirit out of a relationship to Jesus. The Father opened doors to the Gentiles that had, up to that point, been closed. He gave Peter the words to say at that moment, and Peter watched what God was doing as He poured out His Spirit on a people who desired more of Him.

PRAY THIS WITH ME

Father, use us as You will. Let the light of the glory of Christ shine through us in a way that brings honor and glory to Your name. Father, we offer ourselves to You to share and to demonstrate the extravagance of Your love. Father, empower us with Your Holy Spirit through signs, wonders, and miracles. Father, do something through us so large that it can only be accomplished and explained through Your grace and by Your power. Amen!

LET'S TALK ABOUT IT

1. Review the questions in the lesson and discuss your responses.

2. Why was there an emphasis on "doubting nothing"?

3. Why was it important for Peter to cooperate with God in what He was doing?

4. Where did Peter's confidence come from?

5. Why was it important for Peter to obey even if he did not understand all the details?

6. What one thing are you asking the Father to do as a result of this lesson?

Lesson 10

Prayer—The Act of Surrender

⌘

We have been looking at obedience and what that means. Let's turn our attention to surrender. What does it mean to live a surrendered life? What does surrender mean to you? We might say, "I surrendered my life to Christ many years ago," but how does that affect your day-to-day living now? How does that impact our relationships and life events that happen to us?

The prayer of relinquishment is not just an act we do, but a lifestyle we live. It is the posture of heart that depends upon the Lord in and for all things. Many times we hear the word "surrender," and we view it as an act of weakness, giving up, or defeat. We seldom see surrender as an act of victory or living an overcoming life.

The word that strikes the greatest fear in the heart and mind of the believer or the unbeliever is the word "surrender." One of the reasons it strikes such a fear is we believe God will ask us to do something we don't want to do. When we hear the word "surrender," we think of words like acquiescence (a sense of giving in or giving up), weakness, and failure. Another reason we struggle with the word "surrender" is if we don't look out for ourselves, who is going to do that (self is at the center of that statement).

OBSERVATION: Why are we fearful of the word "surrender"?

Could it be that the root of our reluctance to surrender is our distorted view of God? We don't see Him as good or recognize His ability to watch over us—to keep us. We don't believe that His highest desire is for our good.

POWERPOINT: "Surrender" is a powerful word and means something different to each of us. But, relinquishment is the way to live the abundant life. It is the way to live the overcoming, victorious life, and it is the way to live a fruitful and blessed life.

The prayer of submission is aligning our will with God's will. We relinquish our way for His way because His way is higher (Isaiah 55:9). When we see that God is good, we do not need to fear or to be afraid to surrender ourselves to Him.

- Surrender is the most liberating action we can do.
- Yielding is receiving God's will, purpose, and plan for our lives. God's plan for us is good—to give us a future and a hope (Jeremiah 29:11).
- Submitting to God's possibilities, we are living as God intended for us to live.

Years ago E. Stanley Jones, Methodist evangelist and long-time missionary to India in his book, ***Victory Through Surrender,*** defines surrender as that "which seems downward, laying down your arms, is actually a surrender upwards. This is in cooperation with the power that raised

Jesus from the dead—that power, when surrendered to and cooperated with, will raise us from the dead (and everything that separates us from Him—mine). In surrender you align your will to our heavenly Father's will, and you begin to do things you can't do, to accomplish what seems to be impossible." Jones observes, "to surrender is to see that it is the open door to God's everything. You don't have to be worthy, to be deserving; you have to be willing, willing to surrender, not this, that, or the other, but the essential you."

SURRENDER DEFINED

God can keep what we have committed to Him. He holds all things in His hand. He is trustworthy. The disciples knew this as they were threatened by the religious system not to preach or teach about Jesus Christ. They declared, "Lord, You are God, who made heaven and earth and the sea, and all that is in them" (Acts 4:24). We can feel safe and secure in the hands of the One who has created all things, and nothing hidden from His sight. We can live a surrendered life for God is trustworthy and will complete the work He has begun in us. We read that "being confident of this very thing, that He who has begun a good work in you will complete it until the day of Jesus Christ" (Philippians 1:6). Because of God's faithfulness, we do not need to be afraid to surrender all to Jesus.

Abraham was convinced of God's trustworthiness as he was asked by God to sacrifice his son Isaac. When Isaac asked where the sacrifice was, Abraham replied, "My son, God will provide for Himself the lamb for a burnt offering" (Genesis 22:8).

Abraham was confident that even if he surrendered Isaac, God would raise him from the dead, for he knew God was a covenant-keeping God and would not forsake him or let him down, but would keep His promise to Abraham (Hebrew 11:19).

What did surrender mean to Abraham?

Surrender is powerful and causes us to rise above that which would keep us down, discouraged, and defeated.

Submitting ourselves to the Lord releases in us and through us powerful prayer that asks God's intervention and strength. The disciples, when faced with the decision to be bold and powerful witnesses to the resurrection of Jesus Christ, prayed, "Now, Lord, look on their threats, and grant to Your servants that with all boldness they may speak Your word, by stretching out Your hand to heal, and that signs and wonders may be done through the name of Your holy Servant Jesus" (Acts 4:29-30). Surrender is the desire to see God's Kingdom come with power, with love, and with demonstration of His presence.

Yielding to God takes our prayer life to another level. Surrender opens our heart to pray the things that are on God's heart. We begin to ask the Lord to remove those things that prevent us from hearing and doing all He is asking us to do.

Surrender is the way to see things from God's perspective.

The prayer of relinquishment is receiving God's best when it would be easier to accept things as unchangeable, as impossible, and accepting less than God's best and highest will. "And when they had prayed, the place where they were assembled together was shaken; and they were all filled with the Holy Spirit, and they spoke the Word with boldness" (Acts 4:31). Prayer releases the life and power of God not confined by our limited knowledge, wisdom, or ability. When we surrender, we tap into the power of God that enables us to do far more than we could have thought or imagined (Ephesians 3:20). Yielding is exchanging what we cannot do for what God can do when we give ourselves wholly and freely to Him. When we say "yes" to God in surrender to His highest will and purpose, something explosive happens on the inside of us.

Surrendering to Christ's Lordship means:

First of all, we walk in God's highest will. "It is no longer I who live, but Christ lives in me" (Galatians 2:20). When we die to self, we give up all rights to ourselves so that we do not live for ourselves, but for Him who died for us that we might live unto Him. When we walk in surrender to God's highest will and purpose, we are giving ourselves freely and joyfully to all God is so we might receive all that God has for us.

Second, we welcome and receive God's best. "Yet indeed I also count all things loss for the excellence of the knowledge of Christ Jesus my Lord, for whom I have suffered the loss of all things, and count them as rubbish, that I may gain Christ" (Philippians 3:8). We welcome God's best into our lives so Christ may live His life through us.

When we welcome God's presence, we discover the best is yet to come.

Third, we cooperate with Him and His purpose. "Now when they saw the boldness of Peter and John, and perceived that they were uneducated and untrained men, they marveled. And they realized that they had been with Jesus" (Acts 4:13). Surrender is learning to co-labor with Christ to bring the kingdom of God to be a present reality where we are. When we live surrendered lives, the life of Jesus can be seen in us and through us.

People can see we have been with Christ by our desire to remain surrendered to His highest will and purpose.

Waiting is giving away ourselves to God to receive all He has for us as we lay hold of His promises. Surrendering is learning to wait upon the Lord. The very act of surrender itself is waiting upon God to act on our behalf or the behalf of another.

What does surrendering to Christ's Lordship mean to you?

Waiting is an indicator we have surrendered our circumstances and ourselves to God, as we desire His best in our lives. Surrender is "here am I, send me" (Isaiah 6:8).

POWERPOINT: I am learning the best way is the surrendered way. Our hands are open to Him in surrender and commitment. We offer our voice, our mind, our will, our emotions, and our body to Him, and we withhold nothing. Surrender is the place of blessing and fruitfulness.

I am learning relinquishment is receiving God's best and opens doors previously closed. We surrender all we are to all He is, and we can never exhaust who He is and His best for our lives.

Surrender to the keeping power of God (Daniel 6:18-23). Let's look at one person who surrendered himself to the Lord after he learned anyone who did not bow to the king is thrown into the lion's den. The proclamation was a set up by those who were jealous over the insights, understanding, and revelation Daniel walked in (Daniel 6:4b). Therefore, they manipulated king Darius to agree to their scheme without letting him know the hidden motive to get rid of Daniel. They knew he worshiped the Lord and Him only, "Now, O king, establish the decree and sign the writing, so that it cannot be changed, according to the law of the Medes and Persians, which does not alter" (Daniel 6:8).

The decree was "that whoever petitions any god or man for thirty days, except you, O king, shall be cast into the den of lions" (Daniel 6:7b). The king was unaware of the deception that was taking place to harm Daniel. His response to the proclamation was to pray and to seek the face of God, "But when Daniel learned that the law had been signed, he went home and knelt down as usual in his upstairs room, with its windows open toward Jerusalem. He prayed three times a day, just as he had always done, giving thanks to his God" (Daniel 6:10, NLT). When the king received word that Daniel did not obey the edict, it was too late to do anything about it. The king waited anxiously throughout the night as Daniel spent it in the lion's den hoping and believing that no harm would come to him.

> The king spoke, saying to Daniel, "Daniel, servant of the living God, has your God, whom you serve continually, been able to deliver you from the lions?" Then Daniel said to the king, "O king, live forever! My God sent His angel and shut the lions' mouths, so that they have not hurt me, because I was found innocent before Him; and also, O king, I have done no wrong before you" (Daniel 6:20b-22).

What did surrender mean to Daniel?

Abandoning ourselves to the Lord is the way to access all the resources of God.

Surrender is inviting the Lord into where we are, to the things that are happening around us, and our response to those things. Surrender is more than giving our lives to Christ. It is inviting Him to be at the center of all we do and trusting Him to supply us with everything we need. To live above the storm, through the storm, and victorious in the aftermath of what we have just experienced.

Surrender means to submit, relinquish, to hand over, and to yield. The opposite of surrender is to hold out or withhold, to retain, and to resist. We might realize the posture of our hearts to see if we are living the surrendered life by examining these: things we are relinquishing and things we are withholding.

Surrender is a sense of brokenness, to humble ourselves before the Lord. We are asking for His way, not just our way. Surrender is stepping into the power of God, for as long as we do it, we do it in our strength, but when we let

God do it, we step into His power. We are inviting His power to be present and active on our behalf. "But we have this treasure in earthen vessels, that the excellence of the power may be of God and not of us" (2 Corinthians 4:7).

Acquiescence does not mean giving in when the pressure is on. Abdication does not mean giving in to intimidation, fear, or manipulation. To surrender to the Lord is to strengthen ourselves in Him who battles on our behalf.

Those who were seeking to undo Daniel through deceit and trickery knew the practice of Daniel's prayer and devotional life. They waited till they caught him red-handed praying to the God of Israel. They took their findings back to the king and made their case against Daniel. "That Daniel, who is one of the captives from Judah, does not show due regard for you, O king, or for the decree that you have signed, but makes his petition three times a day" (Daniel 6:13).

When our yielding to God is challenged, we can succumb to the pressure of being molded into the image of this world. Or we can surrender to God which speaks of the faith we have in Him to watch over us, keep us, and cause us to overcome that which has come against us. Though the king sought to deliver Daniel, his decree worked against him. Daniel was thrown into the lion's den, but the words of the king became a testimony to the God of Israel whom Daniel served with all his heart, "Your God, whom you serve continually, He will deliver you" (Daniel 6:16b).

Do you think Daniel's time of prayer and devotion escaped the knowledge of the king who knows everything that goes on in his kingdom? Not in the least. The king knew all about his devotion to God, the prayer life he had, and the results that came from spending time with God as the favor of God rested upon Daniel. Is that not the reason he excelled above all the others? It was a long night for the king.

When we stay surrendered, laying our case before the Lord, He will fight on our behalf, and He will bring forth justice and deliver us from that which would do us harm.

Daniel experienced deliverance "because he believed in his God" (Daniel 6:23b). We do not need to be afraid to live our lives surrendered to the Lord when evil seeks to overtake us or when others seek to do us harm. The lies and deception of Daniel's accusers came to light, and truth prevailed. Jesus said, "Whatever you have said in the dark will be heard in the light, and what you have whispered behind closed doors will be shouted from the housetops for all to hear" (Luke 12:3, NLT).

The truth came out and those in collusion, creating a conspiracy against Daniel, came to light. "And the king gave the command, and they brought those men who had accused Daniel, and they cast them into the den of lions—them, their children, and their wives; and the lions overpowered them, and broke all their bones in pieces before they ever came to the bottom of the den" (Daniel 6:24).

Staying surrendered has its challenges and will always be tested. Rest assured that God is able to keep His own who walk in righteousness and who trust in the name of the Lord to deliver, protect, and promote those who are His.

"For He shall give His angels charge over you, to keep you in all your ways" (Psalm 91:11).

Spiritual growth is measured not with human elements like a tape measure, or by a measuring cup, or by weight, but rather, our surrender measures spiritual growth. Surrender conveys trust, faith, openness, vulnerability, and exposure of our heart to the living Lord.

To the degree we are yielded to the Lord is the degree of availability God has to our heart. When we surrender to God's highest will and purpose, the more available we are to Him, and the greater access He has to our heart.

THE POWER OF SURRENDER

God uses all who make themselves available to Him. God is looking for anyone who welcomes the activity of the Holy Spirit to work in and through their lives. God is looking for those who will take Him at His Word: believe it, receive it, and stand upon it until His Word comes to pass in our lives or the lives of others.

Surrender is not just the goal of the Christian life; it is the lifestyle of trusting the Lord in and for all things. Surrender is the way to experience the heart of God.

- Surrender is the place of everlasting joy (Isaiah 35:10).
- Surrender is the place where the power of God keeps us (1 Peter 1:5).
- Surrender is the place of rest (Matthew 11:28).
- Surrender is the place of abiding (John 15:5).

Yielding to God is God getting all of us so that we can experience all of Him.

PRAY THIS WITH ME

Father, You are trustworthy, and we can place ourselves into Your hands and be perfectly at peace as we keep our mind and focus upon You. Father, strengthen us in our inner man to yield ourselves entirely to You. Father, we surrender our will for Your will, and we abandon our way for Your way. We surrender all of ourselves to Your highest will for our lives, and nothing less will do as You keep us as the apple of Your eye. Amen!

LET'S TALK ABOUT IT

1. Review the questions in the lesson and discuss your responses.

2. Why do we struggle with the word "surrender"?

3. What does this statement mean to you: "To surrender is to see that it is the open door to God's everything?"

4. What made Abraham's surrender so powerful? What keeps us from surrendering our all to Christ?

5. How is waiting an indicator that we are surrendered to God?

6. What are you asking the Father to do as a result of this lesson?

Lesson 11

PRAYER—HEALING OF THE WHOLE PERSON

⌘

One of the benefits of the cross is healing and wholeness. The Psalmist writes, "Praise the Lord, my soul, and forget not all his benefits—who forgives all your sins and heals all your diseases" (Psalm 103:2-3, NIV). It is God's will that everyone comes to saving faith in Christ Jesus (John 3:16). He desires that none should perish (2 Peter 3:9). The question becomes why then do we add "if" when we pray for the sick. The phrase "if it is Your will" when praying for the sick never occurs in Scripture. We understand healing is in the atoning work of Jesus on the cross. Does this mean everyone we pray for is healed? Yes, for the work was completed over 2,000 years ago when Jesus hung on the cross for our redemption, our salvation, and our healing. We may not see the manifestation of that healing take place when we pray; however, Jesus answers every prayer. Some prayers are answered immediately, some are progressive, some are partial, and some take place at death—ultimate healing.

> I believe in the power of Jesus Christ to heal the sick and afflicted and to break any bondage when His Name is invoked in any circumstance. I believe His power is as consistently available today as during His own earthly ministry and that, through His Cross,

> He has provided the grounds for us to expect and receive healing and deliverance as surely as we may receive forgiveness and sanctification (Jack Hayford, ***Healing Is for Today***).

Jesus and His disciples had been ministering at the synagogue and encountered a demonized person. Jesus commanded the demonic spirit to be silenced, and He cast it out of the man (Mark 1:23-26). Upon leaving the synagogue, they went to Simon Peter's home for a meal. When they arrived, they discovered Peter's mother-in-law was in bed sick with a fever.

> Now as soon as they had come out of the synagogue, they entered the house of Simon and Andrew, with James and John. But Simon's wife's mother lay sick with a fever, and they told Him about her at once. So He came and took her by the hand and lifted her up, and immediately the fever left her. And she served them (Mark 1:29-31).

We find five truths about her healing:

- She had a need, and Jesus met her at her point of need. "But Simon's wife's mother lay sick with a fever."
- Those present in the house made it known to Jesus about her sickness as an act of intercession, "and they told Him about her at once."
- Jesus came to her and touched her at her point of need. Her fever had made her weak, "so He came and took her by the hand."
- Jesus' power was released as He took her by the hand, "and lifted her up."

- She demonstrated her healing by getting up and serving. "And immediately the fever left her. And she served them."

Which of these five truths spoke to you about Peter's mother-in-law's healing?

For Jesus, healing is not difficult; it flows from His life—Jesus is our Healer (Jehovah-rapha). God says, "For I am the Lord who heals you" (Exodus 15:26). Healing is the very nature and character of God to be the One who brings healing and wholeness to our lives. He heals our brokenness and delivers freedom and completeness. Jesus is our healer, and we are benefactors of God's redemptive plan on the cross and in the resurrection.

There are many dynamics involved that might prevent one's healing and wholeness, as well as a person coming to saving faith in Jesus Christ. We do not throw the baby out with the bathwater by neglecting to pray for the sick. The Bible encourages us to pray for one another that you may be healed (James 5:16) though we may not understand it or believe it. I have learned not to pray "if it is Your will" because I do not find that prayer in Scripture. I want to pray in a way that aligns with the Word of God.

I want to make a strong argument that we are to pray for the sick, for those held captive by sin, and for those who have lived under the oppression of the devil to be set free. We are the redeemed of the Lord, and God uses His people to reconcile others to God (2 Corinthians 5:20).

Part of reconciliation is healing for the whole person. There are three areas that God touches: our soul (mind, will, and emotions), our spirit making us alive unto God, and our body. God is interested in every area of our lives.

He wants the whole person reconciled to Himself. The word "reconcile" is "the reestablishing of a proper, loving, interpersonal relationship, which has been broken or disrupted" ("Word Wealth", p. 1589, ***New Spirit-Filled Life Bible***).

Jesus came and sacrificed His life to reestablish the broken relationship that took place in the Garden and to establish a vital relationship with God, our heavenly Father. Paul explains, "But now in Christ Jesus you who once were far off have been brought near by the blood of Christ" (Ephesians 2:13). You may be asking then how shall we pray? Why is it everyone we pray for is not healed? Why does sickness remain? Good questions.

How does healing happen?

- Healing can be spontaneous (no one prays for them).
- Healing can be progressive and gradual (it is a process).
- Healing can be through doctors and medicine (gifts and talents of others).
- Healing can be instantaneous (all symptoms are gone).
- Healing can be partial (but I believe for more).
- Healing can be seasonal (this too shall pass).
- Healing can be through death (perfect health).

Why is it important to know how healing happens?

These are just some of the reasons why we pray and what happens when we do pray. Healing is not up to us, but up to God for He is our Healer. There are no special formulas we use. Healing is not relegated to a certain few, but all who have a relationship with Jesus can pray for the sick.

We pray a hoped-filled, faith-filled prayer, and we pray with expectation as we stand on the promise of God's Word.

Here is an example of how I have learned to pray:
Lord, I lift Sally to you thanking You for Your presence right here with us. I ask that Sally experience the power of Your presence right now. Thank You that You are Sally's healer and that by Jesus' stripes she has been healed (Isaiah 53:5; 1 Peter 2:24; Matthew 8:17). Father, I ask that You would manifest Your healing upon Sally and demonstrate Your glory. I release her to the ministry of Your Holy Spirit, and I am expecting a good outcome and a good report. Amen!

Let's return to our original questions. Is salvation God's will? Yes! Is healing God's will? Yes! Do all respond to this salvation? No. But, salvation was purchased for us through the sacrificial death of Jesus on the cross. Are all healed? No. But, healing was purchased for us through the sacrificial death of Jesus on the cross.

Therefore, we pray all come to know Jesus personally, and we pray all walk in healing and wholeness and experience the freedom that only Christ can give (John 8:36). We experience healing and wholeness through God's redemptive plan for Planet Earth. "In Him we have redemption through His blood, the forgiveness of sins, according to the riches of His grace" (Ephesians 1:7). Redemption means "deliverance through Christ from evil and the penalty of sin. The price paid to purchase that liberation was His shed blood" ("Word Wealth," p. 1554, ***New Spirit-Filled Life Bible***).

God's redemptive plan for the world:

- Christ loves us infinitely. His love for us will never diminish.
- Christ died on the cross for us (salvation, healing, wholeness—spirit, soul, and body).
- Christ calls us to co-labor with Him to bring heaven to earth. Is there sickness in heaven? NO!
- Christ has given us truths, promises, and the revelation about Himself by which we can pray for others.
- Christ has instructed us to pray faith-filled prayers, for without faith it is impossible to please Him. "Faith is the substance of things hoped for, the conviction of things not seen" (Hebrews 11:6). God honors the simplicity of faith and trust.
- We know amid a fallen world. Jesus always has the last word and that He sits on the throne ruling and reigning forever. Jesus broke into a fallen world and offered Himself as the eternal sacrifice for sins, past, present, and future and reconciled us to God.

Describe in your own words God's redemptive plan for the world.

POWERPOINT: When we say "if" before or after our prayer, we tend to blame God and to accuse Him. If that person is not healed then God is at fault, and we become angry. When we pray prayers of release, blessing, wholeness, with expectation, and laying hold of the promises of God, we advance the kingdom of God where we are.

There are still mysteries when it comes to healing of the whole person that may always remain a mystery until we get to heaven. At that time, it is no longer an issue for us. But we live now with the tension between this world and seeing God's Kingdom come and His redemptive plan realized fully in this life. It demands that we provide a place, an opportunity, and a faith-filled community who pray and believe God's glory to be experienced and for His Kingdom to become a present reality.

PRAYER—THE DETERMINING FACTOR

> Because I believe through the atoning and redemptive work of Jesus on the cross and the shedding of His blood for our salvation. I accept the ministry of healing as a part of the Lord Jesus Christ's commission that the Church go to the whole world with the Gospel. This includes proclaiming God's will and power to heal, and in Jesus' Name that the prayer of faith be offered, confession of sins be made unto deliverance, elders anoint with oil, and hands be laid on the sick that they may recover. I believe in the power of God's Word and Spirit to sustain and supply health to those who walk simply and humbly before Him in

> faith. I believe the fruit of such faith will be manifest in love and patience (Jack Hayford, Article: "Healing Is For Today").

Let us conclude our study on prayer and healing of the whole person by looking at Mark 2:3-12. Jesus is in Capernaum teaching the Word in a house that was full, and the crowd overflowed to outside. Four men wanted to bring their friend to Jesus for healing, but there was no room for them, so they looked for another way to bring their friend to Jesus.

JESUS FORGIVES AND HEALS A PARALYTIC

> Then they came to Him, bringing a paralytic who was carried by four men. And when they could not come near Him because of the crowd, they uncovered the roof where He was. So when they had broken through, they let down the bed on which the paralytic was lying. When Jesus saw their faith, He said to the paralytic, "Son, your sins are forgiven you." And some of the scribes were sitting there and reasoning in their hearts, "Why does this Man speak blasphemies like this? Who can forgive sins but God alone?" But immediately, when Jesus perceived in His spirit that they reasoned thus within themselves, He said to them, "Why do you reason about these things in your hearts? Which is easier, to say to the paralytic, 'Your sins are forgiven you,' or to say, 'Arise, take up your bed and walk'? But that you may know that the Son of Man has power on earth to forgive sins"—He said to the paralytic, "I say to you, arise, take up your bed, and go to your house."

> Immediately he arose, took up the bed, and went out in the presence of them all, so that all were amazed and glorified God, saying, "We never saw anything like this!" (Mark 2:1-12).

FOUR MEN WHO REFUSED TO GIVE UP

First of all, these men pressed through when it would have been easier to walk away. "Soon the house where He was staying was so packed with visitors that there wasn't room for one more person, not even outside the door. And He preached the word to them" (Mark 2:2, NLT).

POWERPOINT: This is the pivotal point in the story Mark is describing. If the men had allowed discouragement to overcome them, they would have walked away. If they had become disillusioned, they would have become critical and cynical. They refused to become discouraged or cynical. They chose to press through all the objections, obstacles, and distractions because they would not be denied their opportunity to bring their friend to Christ.

They were willing to do whatever it took. Jesus said, "The Law and the prophets were until John. Since that time the Kingdom of God has been preached, and everyone is pressing into it" (Luke 16:16). These men were pressing to see the manifestation of the kingdom of God to become a present reality for their friend.

These men carrying their paralytic friend could have said, "*There is no way to get to Jesus. The house is too crowded.*" Or they could have said, "*We'll come back later*," but by that time Jesus could have moved on to another place. The question was how badly did they want it? Were they willing to make the sacrifices needed to find a way? Would they walk away thinking about what could have been?

Secondly, these men sought to find a place of entrance into His presence. "They couldn't get to Jesus through the crowd, so they dug through the clay roof above His head…" (Mark 2:4, NLT). Isaiah exhorts the people, "Go through, go through the gates [place of entrance]! Prepare the way for the people...take out the stones, lift up a banner for the peoples!" (Isaiah 62:10). These men went to another level of prayer and intercession for their friend. They said, *"We'll tear the roof off the house, and we will create a gate, a window, a portal, an entrance to the presence of Christ."* They were creating a place for God to use. They were removing obstacles that might keep them from His presence, "So when they had broken through" (Mark 2:4). Mark declares, not "if" they could break through, but "when" they broke through. I see this as intercession on the part of the four men who brought their friend into the presence of Jesus.

Finally, these men demonstrated faith. "Then they lowered the sick man on his mat, right down in front of Jesus. Seeing their faith, Jesus said to the paralyzed man…" (Mark 2:4b-5, NLT).

They could have formed a committee—a task force—and studied the situation and examined all their options. They could have voted on which one to go with and still be left holding their paralyzed friend with his unmet need. When there is a sense of urgency—faith and action are required.

There are times when the clock of eternity is ticking away, and our opportunities become smaller and smaller. If not now, when?

When facing obstacles and barriers, will we press into the presence of Christ at all cost? When it seems that there is no room, will we determine to seek Christ's presence and bring our need before Him? When it appears that there is no room, will we refuse to deviate from the mission and plan God has put within our hearts? So what is it that creates that place of entrance, that place that brings us into the presence of God? Faith—faith working through love.

These men activated their faith:

- They were relentless in pressing through the obstacles that stood between them and Jesus, between their barrier and their miracle.
- Their radical faith did not go unnoticed. Jesus saw their faith (Hebrews 11:6).
- The reassuring words of Jesus gave them hope as Jesus spoke words of healing and restoration to their friend. "Son, your sins are forgiven you...Arise, take up your bed and walk" (Mark 2:5b, 9b).
- Their faith released a miracle to the congregation gathered in that home. The people raised their voice in praise to God as they "were amazed and glorified God, saying, 'We never saw anything like this'" (Mark 2: 12b).

Which one of these four ways of this activated faith spoke to you?

We noted earlier there could be reasons we have not received our healing. Could it be this paralyzed man needed first to know his sins were forgiven then followed by his healing? There may be some things in our lives for which we need to receive God's forgiveness, or maybe we need to forgive those who have wounded us before we experience the healing for which we have been praying come to pass.

The church was never the same after that day as they witnessed this miracle. "The man jumped up, took the mat, and pushed his way through the stunned onlookers" (Mark 2:12, NLT).

Terry Teykl, in his book ***The Presence Based Church,*** well describes what went on that day, "The presence of God overflowed onto unsuspecting worshipers that day. Like holy lava cascading down the sides of a volcano, the essence of God's holiness, power, love, and grace were evident to all in the house."

God does not leave us half-healed. He is the One who heals us and makes us whole. Our healing may come quickly, or it may be over a process of time. What we do know, however, is that healing comes through faith standing firm upon the promises of God and His ability to keep us in all circumstances of life. He is called Faithful and True (Revelation 19:11) and will never leave us or forsake us.

This chapter has been about the healing of the whole person. The purpose is to whet your appetite to explore this area more fully and to begin praying for one another that we may be healed. To pray for the sick and one another is one of the most loving and compassionate things we can do.

Suggestions of some ways to offer healing in our churches:

- Plan a healing service. This can be once a month or a planned time in the worship service.
- When serving Holy Communion, provide an opportunity to pray for the sick.
- Train a group of folks to visit the hospital and pray for the sick.
- Provide "prayer cloths" to give away to family, friends, co-workers as a point of contact for healing.
- Provide training opportunities to equip folks to be agents of healing and blessing. Select a book on healing and study it in a small group setting.

LET'S TALK ABOUT IT

1. Why is it easier to pray for someone's salvation than to believe for one's healing?

2. According to Psalm 103:2-3, what are our benefits?

3. What spoke to you the most about the healing of Peter's mother-in-law?

4. What does it mean to press into God for our need?

5. What spoke to you the most about the healing of the paralyzed man brought to Jesus by his friends?

6. What role does faith take in praying for the sick?

7. How can we provide opportunities in our churches to offer healing services or to become a center for healing?

8. What is one thing you are asking God to take away from this lesson?

Lesson 12

PRAYING AGAINST STRONGHOLDS

⌘

VICTIM OR VICTORIOUS

Jesus was back in Jerusalem after spending two days in Galilee and traveled over to Cana where He had turned water into wine. There He ministered to the son of a government official from the city of Capernaum (John 4:43f). Jesus approached the Sheep Gate, called Bethesda in Hebrew. The pool, surrounded by five porches, was where those with diseases, illnesses, and sicknesses would gather for healing and wholeness. When the angel came down and stirred the water, the one who reached the pool first would receive their healing. There was a man who been trapped in his prison of sickness for thirty-eight years until Jesus offered him a way out (John 5:1-15).

When Jesus saw him lying there and knew he already had been in that condition a long time, He said to him, "Do you want to be made well?" (John 5:6).

> The sick man answered Him, "Sir, I have no man to put me into the pool when the water is stirred up; but while I am coming, another steps down before me." Jesus said to him, "Rise, take up your bed and walk." And immediately the man was made well, took up his

bed, and walked. And that day was the Sabbath (John 5:7-9).

What is a stronghold?

DEALING WITH STRONGHOLDS

This paralytic man was living under a stronghold when he began to experience Christ's freedom. His breakthrough was coming, but Jesus wanted to know if he wanted to be free or not. This man had been living in a stronghold of defeat, despair, and hopelessness. He knew there was no way to get out of the cave in which he was living (emotionally, mentally, physically, and spiritually).

A stronghold is anything that has a strong hold on us. It can be good or bad. The Psalmist declared, "The Lord is a stronghold for the oppressed, a stronghold in times of trouble" (Psalm 9:9, ESV). On the other hand, Gideon was instructed by the Lord to tear down the altar of Baal. "Build an altar to the Lord your God on the top of the stronghold here" (Judges 6:26, ESV).

We pull down the strongholds that oppose the purpose, plan, and will of God. We establish the Lordship of Jesus in those areas of our lives in which we need His touch and freedom.

The Bible would not have spoken of strongholds if it were not a possibility for them to exist. Jesus is our door to freedom, healing, and wholeness.

STRONGHOLDS DEFINED

In his book ***Prevailing in the Battle Zone***, Rob McCorkle defines a stronghold as "a Castle, fortress or citadel embedded in arguments."

Author Ed Silvoso defines a spiritual stronghold as "a mind-set impregnated with hopelessness that causes us to accept as unchangable, situations that we know are contrary to the will of God" (***That None Should Perish***).

Beth Moore offers this definition:

> A stronghold is anything that exalts itself in our minds, "pretending" to be bigger or more powerful than our God. It steals much of our focus and causes us to feel overpowered. Controlled. Mastered. Whether the stronghold is an addiction, unforgiveness toward a person who has hurt us, or despair over a loss, it is something that consumes so much of our emotional and mental energy that abundant life is strangled (Terry Teykl, ***Divine Strongholds***).

POWERPOINT: The truth is we can occupy a place in God and never experience the depth of His mercy and grace—the outpouring of His extravagant love and affection—that He has for us. Sometimes we hold the Lord at bay and are never really able to embrace His mercy and grace with the outpouring of love and affection.

How many times do you think this man got his hopes up only to be disappointed once again? The man built a stronghold of defeat, despair, and hopelessness and had a litany of arguments. He had built a ceiling over his head and could not see beyond the limitations under which he lived.

These are the strongholds—arguments—that kept this man captive (John 5:7, NLT):

- "*I can't, sir.*" This was an excuse he learned to give.
- He had become enslaved by his circumstances. "For I have no one to put me into the pool when the water bubbles up."
- It seems as if self-pity had set in. "*Someone else always gets in ahead of me.*"

What kept this man captive for so many years? When did he decide things could be different?

Jesus asked this man one of the most profound questions, "Do you want to be made well?" That is, "*Are you serious about this—how badly do you want to be made well?*" Sometimes it is easier to remain where we are than to embrace the new thing God wants to do.

The man immediately responded for he had conditioned himself on what to say and had well-rehearsed in his mind why things could not change, would never change, and why his circumstances were forever unchangeable.

BREAKING STRONGHOLDS

God gives us supernatural strength to break through the barriers that keep us enslaved. The Word says, "For I can do everything with the help of Christ who gives me the strength I need" (Philippians 4:13, NLT).

Strongholds are broken when we believe the truth of God's Word and not the lies of the enemy. Jesus prays for His disciples that the Father would "make them holy by your truth; teach them your word, which is truth" (John 17:17, NLT).

The breakthrough comes when we begin to lift our voices. Isaiah declares that the enemy, the Assyrian army, "runs at the sound of your voice" (Isaiah 33:3). We speak and declare, as the children of God, that the enemy flees at the sound of our voice. For it is the voice of authority—the voice of victory.

The Lord is our light in dark places. Jesus is the One who is the stronghold of our lives and will never let us go. "He has enabled you to share in the inheritance that belongs to his people, who live in the light. For he rescued us from the kingdom of darkness and transferred us into the kingdom of his dear son" (Colossians 1:12-13, NLT). The paralytic's breakthrough was coming. Jesus wanted to know if he wanted to be free or not.

THE WAY OF FREEDOM

First, we discover the way of freedom was the place of God's empowering grace. Jesus said, "Stand up, pick up your mat, and walk!" (John 5:8, NLT). Following his list of arguments, which were the strongholds in his life, Jesus commanded him to do something. It is hard to do something when you have been in the same place practically all your life.

At some point, the empowering grace of God gives us the ability to walk out of what has held us down all our lives. "And immediately the man was made well, took up his bed, and walked" (John 5:9). We find in Mark 2:9 that Jesus addresses the paralytic, "Arise, take up your bed and walk." Again, something was required of that man to pick up what had been holding him down and to receive the gracious words of Jesus to rise and walk.

What did the empowering grace of God mean to this man who had been in the "cave" for thirty-eight years?

He had to be willing to leave behind where he had lived for thirty-eight years. What will life be like on the outside? He had to learn to think differently about his life and his future. He would be asking, "*What am I going to do with the rest of my life?*" He had to believe larger than he had previously thought.

What will a life of faith require of him? God redeems situations by bringing present hope to the place of previous defeat, despair, and hopelessness. It was a time of repentance, of changing his mind, about how he was going to live for the rest of his life.

Second, we discover the way of freedom to be a place of overcoming. But afterward, Jesus found him in the temple probably said, "*Now you are well; so stop sinning*" (John 5:14).

To the woman caught in adultery, Jesus said, "Go and sin no more" (John 8:11). To the paralyzed man in the book of Mark, Jesus said, "Your sins are forgiven you" (Mark 2:5, 9).

Jesus became the paralytic man's:

- Living water stirring within him.
  "Whoever desires, let him take the water of life freely" (Revelation 22:17b). He would no longer need to wait for the stirring of the water for Jesus became living water for him.
- Hope to the hopeless.
  "Now may the God of hope fill you with all joy and peace in believing, that you may abound in hope by the power of the Holy Spirit" (Romans 15:13). For the first time in this man's life, hope was rising. Victory came to a man who lived defeated and believed that his case was unchangeable. "And this is the victory that has overcome the world—our faith" (1 John 5:4b).

Jesus changes what seems to be unchangeable when it seems our fate is fixed.

JESUS RESTORES LIFE

He restores what the enemy meant for evil and destruction. "Yet when he is found, he must restore sevenfold; He may have to give up all the substance of his house" (Proverbs 6:31).

He restores our joy when circumstances have weighed us down. "Restore to me the joy of Your salvation, and uphold me by Your generous Spirit" (Psalm 51:12).

He restores health. "'For I will restore health to you and heal you of your wounds,' says the LORD" (Jeremiah 30:17).

Lastly, we discover the way of freedom shows the compassion of Jesus. "When He saw the multitudes, He was moved with compassion for them, because they were weary and scattered, like sheep having no shepherd" (Matthew 9:36). There is something inside that moves us out of our complacency and passivity to passion and ministry to those who are not yet in Christ. It is the Spirit of God that arrests us, and we have become captive to Him so that our heart beats with His heart. We have the heart of God for the world; we long for the world to know Christ personally. The phrase "moved with compassion" means the place where we feel genuinely and are moved by the love of God to feel as He feels.

We are moved with compassion for those who are bound in a stronghold of sin, fear, and unbelief. We feel genuinely for people who are hurting and desperately need the touch of Christ. We feel for those who have built walls around themselves so they will never be hurt again. We feel genuinely for those who are sick, ill, and live in constant pain—those who long for relief and desire desperately the healing touch of Christ. We feel deeply for the hearts and lives broken because of anger, resentment, bitterness, and need the touch of Jesus who heals the brokenhearted and sets free those oppressed by demonic forces.

Author Jack Deere observes, "To the degree that we can enter into His compassion for the sick and for the hurting, we can be vessels (of mercy) through whom the healing power of Jesus can flow" (***Surprised By the Power of the Spirit).***

Paul observes, "And have put on the new man who is renewed in knowledge according to the image of Him who created him" (Colossians 3:10). The word "renew" means a renovation, restoration, transformation, and a change of heart and life. It indicates an adjustment of one's moral and spiritual vision, and this is the work of the Holy Spirit in us.

What does it mean to have our mind renewed?
How does this happen?

In His presence, we discover a new way to live, a new way to walk, a new way to think, and a new way to believe.

POWERPOINT: God desires to do something deep within our heart, to change our perspective about life and our view of who He is. God wants to change our view of ourselves and others. God is our all-sufficient One who meets us where we are and does something radical, transformational, and powerful in us and through us.

PRAY THIS WITH ME

Father, You are the One who sets the captive free. Father, we desire to walk in that freedom and experience Your peace and joy. Father, break off any area in our lives in which there is a stronghold that keeps us from following You with all our heart. Father, let the river of Your Spirit flow through us powerfully and fruitfully. Father, through Your empowering grace, we will live an overcoming life. Father, remove the things that hinder our knowing You and Your ability to touch us at our deepest need and to experience the freedom that only Your can give. Amen!

LET'S TALK ABOUT IT

1. Review the questions in the lesson and discuss your responses.

2. What is a stronghold?

3. How does a stronghold infiltrate our lives?

4. What does it mean that a stronghold is a mind-set impregnated with hopelessness? Why must we have our minds renewed?

5. Why was this man who had been sick for 38 years reluctant to receive his healing?

6. How can we experience the freedom that only Christ can give?

7. How can we show compassion for those entangled in strongholds?

8. What are you asking the Father to do as a result of this lesson?

Lesson 13

Prophetic Prayer—
Releasing the Purpose of God

⌘

Throughout this study, we have been preparing ourselves to pray prophetically. To pray prophetically is to come boldly before the Lord and make strong requests. To pray prophetically is to listen to the voice of God and begin to pray what we hear Him saying. To pray prophetically is to declare and decree the Word of God over a person, place, or event. We begin to pray what Jesus taught His disciples to pray, "Our Father in heaven, Hallowed be Your name. Your Kingdom come. Your will be done on earth as it is in heaven" (Matthew 6:9-10).

POWERPOINT: Prophetic praying is declaring the things in heaven to become a present reality where we are. Prophetic praying releases heaven upon the earth—upon persons, places, and events.

PRAYING THE WORD OF GOD

I believe praying the Word of God assists us in praying prophetically. Therefore, to pray prophetically is to pray His Word. We decree things to be done on earth as it is in heaven and for God to bring forth His purpose. Recently, I have been asking the Lord to teach me to pray larger prayers—to pray boldly, courageously, and audaciously.

Along with that, I have been asking the Lord to teach me to pray in such a way that releases the things of heaven waiting to be released upon the earth.

There are some things God will not disclose, release, or reveal until we begin to release those things upon the earth. There are times God will not act until we take the initiative to pray. There are yet things to be discovered as God waits for us to pray those things to come to pass. There are songs, books, and inventions waiting to be released, but God is waiting for us to release those things upon the earth through prayer. Prophetic praying flows out of intimacy with the Lord. It comes from staying in His presence as we abide in Him daily—looking to Him, the Author and Perfector of our faith (Hebrews 12:2).

HEARING THE VOICE OF GOD

Prophetic praying is waiting upon God and listening to His voice. We begin to articulate the promises of God to come upon persons, places, and events. We desire the Father's heart to be revealed, released, and experienced upon the earth, and upon earthen vessels (2 Corinthians 4:7).

POWERPOINT: To pray prophetically is to speak to the mountains in our lives or the lives of others. It is to speak to the chaos and declare the peace of God in our lives or the lives of others. It is to speak to the barren places and declare life and fruitfulness.

Isaiah the prophet gives us this insight about speaking prophetically over those the barren places, "Until the Spirit is poured upon us from on high, and the wilderness becomes a fruitful field and the fruitful field is counted as a forest" (Isaiah 32:15). We declare the purpose of God to come forth and pray until we get a breakthrough. We declare the Spirit of God to be poured out upon the dry places, the barren places, and the lifeless places. God is waiting for someone to speak His Word, to declare His purpose, and to stand upon His promises. Will we be the ones to do that?

LIFE IN THE VALLEY

Ezekiel was brought to a valley full of bones that were strewed out across the land. God's instruction to Ezekiel was to speak to the bones (Ezekiel 37). You have to wonder what was going through Ezekiel's mind as he looked and saw the disarray, the disorder, and the jumbled mess that filled the land.

What would it take for Ezekiel to speak to the bones? What did he see in his heart and mind that up until that time looked impossible? What rose up within Ezekiel to declare the Word of the Lord over such a mass of confusion and barrenness? Where did the courage and boldness originate for him to speak such a large, bold, and audacious prayer? It came from the Spirit of God to see what he had not seen before, to believe larger than he could have thought earlier, and to speak words that released life.

We can release life-giving words for the life of the Son of God resides and rests upon us. Paul writes:

> "Eye has not seen, nor ear heard, nor have entered into the heart of man the things which God has

> prepared for those who love Him." But God has revealed them to us through His Spirit. For the Spirit searches all things, yes, the deep things of God (1 Corinthians 2:9-10).

We speak and declare the things God has for us to come forth in the Name of Jesus.

What enabled Ezekiel to see what God was showing him?

LED BY THE SPIRIT

The first thing we find God initiated is this plan of action for Ezekiel to speak to the bones, "The hand of the Lord came upon me and brought me out in the Spirit of the Lord, and set me down in the midst of the valley; and it was full of bones" (Ezekiel 37:1). The hand of God is upon us, and His Spirit is in us, and He wants to do something through us so amazing that the only explanation is He did it. The prophet Zechariah had a Word from the Lord to Zerubbabel, the Governor of Judah, concerning the rebuilding of the temple saying it would be done "not by might nor by power, but by My Spirit" (Zechariah 4:6).

When God is about to do something, He shows us the reality of things and says something like, *"There is more to be done, and I am going to show you things I will do through you if you will obey My Word and begin doing what seems to be impossible."*

ACTION IS REQUIRED

Ezekiel was snatched away and taken to a certain place through the Spirit's leading, and he began to see things from God's perspective. "Then He caused me to pass by them all around, and behold, there were very many in the open valley; and indeed they were very dry. And He said to me, 'Son of man, can these bones live?'" (Ezekiel 37:2-3a). God allows us to see things as they are. Concerning the things we are facing, the things we have experienced, the things we have lost, and the things we have laid aside, He may ask us *"Can life come again? Can hope arise out of the ashes? Can order come out of chaos? Can what you have experienced be turned around?"* God always asks us questions that provoke the heart, that cause us to look at something again, and a grain of hope is planted in the heart and is watered by the Holy Spirit.

A WORD IN SEASON

God continued to press Ezekiel as he saw the bones spread across the land. God said again to Ezekiel:

> "Prophesy to these bones, and say to them, 'O dry bones, hear the word of the Lord! Thus says the Lord God to these bones: "Surely I will cause breath to enter into you, and you shall live"'"(Ezekiel 37:4-5).

After we have seen things from God's perspective and hope rises within us, the Spirit of the Lord encourages us, and we are able to speak life. We speak resurrection to that which is dead.

If we don't release life-giving Words of God to what seems to be unchangeable circumstances, who will? Who will speak to what appears to be setbacks we can't recover from that have bested us? If we don't speak to that which seems to be a mess, filled with disorder and chaos, who will? If we don't initiate heaven's desire, who will?

WORDS OF LIFE

The writer of Proverbs observes how powerful our words are, "Death and life are in the power of the tongue, and those who love it will eat its fruit" (Proverbs 18:21). We speak life because we enjoy the fruit of speaking life, blessing, health, healing, and wholeness into persons, places, and events.

Ezekiel was charged to speak on God's behalf to the bones—to the crisis. Prophesying is speaking on behalf of God what He desires to do that we cannot do on our own. Prophesying on God's behalf requires we learn to hear His voice and to obey the things we hear Him say. We speak words that build up, encourage, edify, and are life-giving (1 Corinthians 14:3). All of us can pray prophetic prayers as we speak on behalf of God. Our voice may be the only voice of God that others may hear; therefore, we speak.

> So I prophesied as I was commanded; and as I prophesied, there was a noise, and suddenly a rattling; and the bones came together, bone to bone. Indeed, as I looked, the sinews and the flesh came upon them, and the skin covered them over; but there was no breath in them. Also He said to me, "Prophesy to the breath, prophesy, son of man, and

> say to the breath, 'Thus says the Lord God: "Come from the four winds, O breath, and breathe on these slain, that they may live."'" So I prophesied as He commanded me, and breath came into them, and they lived, and stood upon their feet, an exceedingly great army (Ezekiel 37:7-10).

WORDS TO OBEY

We not only desire to hear the voice of God, but we also want to follow what He is saying even though at the moment it seems impossible and entirely ridiculous. We are not moved by what we see; we are only moved by what we hear the Lord saying. We leave the results to Him.

Ezekiel did what he was commanded to do—no less, no more. We begin to speak words of life, healing, freedom, restoration, renewing, and wholeness over people, places and events, and watch what the Lord will do. As we obey the Words of the Lord, we are not only cooperating with God's purpose, we are also co-laboring with Him in releasing heaven upon earth.

POWERPOINT: *Lord Jesus, teach us to pray prayers that release things in heaven ready to be released, and we release those things through prophetic prayers.*

WORDS OF HOPE AND PROMISE

Ezekiel spoke to the winds for the breath of God to come and fill the emptiness, the void, the chaos, and the barrenness. God did so and raised an exceedingly great army (Ezekiel 37:9-10). We look through our natural eyes and see things as impossible, hopeless, and unchangeable. God sees something entirely different because with Him nothing is impossible (Matthew 17:20). There is life in our voices because the presence of God resides in us, and we speak what is inside us to come forth with blessing, healing, and wholeness. Where there has been fracture, brokenness, and destruction, we speak life. Paul writes, "Let no corrupt word proceed out of your mouth, but what is good for necessary edification, that it may impart grace to the hearers" (Ephesians 4:29). The word "corrupt" means decay, rotten as used to describe spoiled meat or rotten fruit.

> Then He said to me, "Son of man, these bones are the whole house of Israel. They indeed say, 'Our bones are dry, our hope is lost, and we ourselves are cut off!' Therefore prophesy and say to them, 'Thus says the Lord God: "Behold, O My people, I will open your graves and cause you to come up from your graves, and bring you into the land of Israel. Then you shall know that I am the Lord, when I have opened your graves, O My people, and brought you up from your graves. I will put My Spirit in you, and you shall live, and I will place you in your own land. Then you shall know that I, the Lord, have spoken it and performed it," says the Lord'" (Ezekiel 37:11-14).

THE WITNESS OF THE SPIRIT

God is the God of resurrection and brings us out of our graves of despair and defeat. "Behold, O My people, I will open your graves and cause you to come up from your graves" (Ezekiel 37:12b). God identifies us as His people whom He brought from death to life, and He calls us His sons and daughters. It is the Lord who liberates and puts a new step in our walk with Him. God puts His Spirit in us, and we come alive. "But if the Spirit of Him who raised Jesus from the dead dwells in you, He who raised Christ from the dead will also give life to your mortal bodies through His Spirit who dwells in you" (Romans 8:11). God told Ezekiel He would put His Spirit in these bones and would raise a mighty army.

WE ALL CAN PRAY PROPHETICALLY

Every believer can declare the Word of the Lord over persons, places, and events that bring life, healing, and freedom. We speak what we hear as Jesus instructed us, "Whatever I tell you in the dark, speak in the light; and what you hear in the ear, preach on the housetops" (Matthew 10:27). We found earlier, to speak prophetically is to speak on behalf of God. What we hear Him saying in the quiet times, we speak life-giving words that bring light, liberty, freedom, and healing.

POWERPOINT: To prophesy means to speak on God's behalf. It also means to give shape to, or to give form, as laying a foundation upon which to build. It is giving structure where there is no structure or foundation, where there is chaos and to bring shape, form, and purpose. When we speak God's life-giving Words, we bring shape, structure, and purpose to people, places, and events.

Ezekiel obeyed the Lord as he spoke to the dry bones that were disjointed, lifeless, and barren, and a foundation of life was beginning to come together. The Lord was constructing a great army filled with purpose. In essence, what Ezekiel was speaking and declaring was giving shape to God's people to fulfill His purpose. "Then you shall know that I, the Lord, have spoken it and performed it," says the Lord" (Ezekiel 37:14b). The Lord wanted everyone to know that it was He who raised this exceedingly great army to fulfill His purpose.

We can all pray prophetically:

- Moses declared, "Oh, that all the Lord's people were prophets and that the Lord would put His Spirit upon them" (Numbers 11:29b).
- We can all hear the voice of God. "My sheep hear My voice, and I know them, and they follow Me" (John 10:27).
- God has given us His Spirit. "The Spirit Himself bears witness with our spirit that we are children of God" (Romans 8:16).
- We can all speak words of encouragement, exhortation, and comfort (1 Corinthians 14:3). We can speak life-giving words.
- God's anointing rests upon us. "But you have an anointing from the Holy One, and you know all things" (1 John 2:20).
- God has given us His Spirit that we might know what He freely gives us. "Now we have received, not the spirit of the world, but the Spirit who is from God, that we might know the things that have been freely given to us by God" (1 Corinthians 2:12).
- We have been made in the image of God. God spoke, and life came forth. We speak, and life is released upon that which is barren, fruitless, and to that which

holds us captive. Paul writes, "That I may open my mouth boldly to make known the mystery of the gospel" (Ephesians 6:19b).

- With all boldness, we proclaim and declare the Word of the Lord over persons, places, and events because we have been given authority. If we don't do it, who will? May the Lord give us His words to speak healing, restoration, and freedom. The Lord is waiting to act for those who pray.

Why can we pray prophetic prayers?
What does this mean to us today?

Let us be the answer to Moses' prayer, that all God's people be prophetic (Number 11:29). May the Holy Spirit stir within us the prophetic voice that brings encouragement, comfort, and build one another in our faith. We can all prophesy and speak the Word of the Lord that brings life where there is death, to speak hope where there is hopelessness, and we speak words that encourage to all who are discouraged and downcast. Will we arise as the sons and daughters of God who bring the Word of the Lord to this generation?

LET'S TALK ABOUT IT

1. Review the questions in the lesson and discuss your responses.

2. What is prophetic prayer?

3. What was Ezekiel instructed to do to the bones?

4. What does it mean that action is needed when praying prophetically?

5. When we pray prophetically, what are we speaking?

6. What does the word "prophesy" mean? How is this related to praying prophetically?

7. What area in our lives do we need to begin speaking words of life, healing, freedom, and victory?

8. What are you asking the Father to do as a result of this lesson?

About the Author

RAY PETTY has served in pastoral ministry for over 37 years. He has pioneered and pastored churches, taught in Bible schools, directed Christian education, and organized life-changing small groups in the United States. Pastor Ray has been personally impacted by small group ministry and focuses on this solid way to develop disciples, grow leaders, and multiply the church. Ray is the author of ***Journey in Discipleship Study Guide***, ***Going Beyond Study Guide***, and ***Teach Us to Pray Study Guide***. He received his Masters of Divinity from Asbury Theological Seminary and his bachelor's degree from Oral Roberts University. Ray is a husband, father, and grandfather; he lives in Tennessee with his wife, Alice.

Addendum

Ways to develop a prayer ministry:

- Study a book together that assists in learning and developing a prayer ministry.
- Have opportunity during a communion service to pray for the sick.
- Develop a prayer room (for people to come and pray during the week and to gather before the worship service).
- Provide a healing service once a month.
- Expect signs of the presence of Jesus to become more evident.
- Develop home groups where study and prayer can take place.
- Begin to identify those who have a passion for praying.
- Make prayer a priority in your personal life and the life of the church.

Bibliography

Campbell, Wesley, Welcoming a Visitation of the Holy Spirit, Charisma House, Lake Mary, FL, 1996.

Copeland, Germaine, Prayers That Avail Much, Harrison House, Tulsa, OK, 1997.

Damazio, Frank, The Attitude of Faith, Whitaker House, Portland, OR, 2009.

Deere, Jack, Surprised By the Power of the Spirit, Zondervan Publishing, 1993.

Duewell, Wesley L., Mighty Prevailing Prayer, Zondervan Publishing House, 1990.

Frangipane, Francis, This Day We Fight, Chosen Books, Grand Rapids, MI, 2005.

Foster, Richard, Celebration of Discipline, Harper & Collins, New York, NY, 1978.

Hayford, Jack, Ebook: Healing Is For Today, Xlibris Corporation, Bloomington, IN, 2001.

Jacobs Cindy, The Power of Persistent Prayer, Bethany House, Minneapolis, MI, 2011.

Johnson, Bill, When Heaven Invades Earth, Destiny Image, Shippensburg, PA, 2003.

Jones, E. Stanley, Victory Through Surrender, Abingdon Press, Nashville, TN, 1966.

McCorkle, Rob, Prevailing in the Battle Zone, Fire School Ministries Publication, Groveport, OH, 2015.

Morgan, G. Campbell, The Welch Revival, (London, 1905; Reprint in The Watchman, 1905)

Murray, Andrew, God's Best Secrets, Zondervan Publishing House, 1950.

Munroe, Myles, Understanding Your Place in the God's Kingdom, Destiny Image, Shippensburg, PA, 2011.

New Spirit-Filled Life Bible, Thomas Nelson, Nashville, TN, 2002.

Pierce, Chuck, Time To Defeat The Devil, Charisma House, Lake Mary, FL, 2011.

Rutland, Mark, Launch Out Into The Deep, Bristol Books, Hayward, CA, 1987.

Silvoso, Ed, That None Should Perish, Chosen Grand Rapids, MI, 1994.

Slaughter, Michael, Unlearning Church, Group Publishing, Inc., Loveland, CO, 2002.

Sorge, Bob, Secrets of the Secret place, Oasis House, Kansas City, Missouri, 2012.H

Teykl, Terry, Divine Strongholds, Prayer Point Press, Muncie, IN, 2008.

Teykl, Terry, The Presence Based Church, Prayer Point Press, Muncie, IN, 2003.

Parsons Publishing House
Your Voice Your World™

GOING BEYOND—STUDY GUIDE

From Your Path of Disappointment to God's Overcoming Love

Have you ever experienced setbacks, failures, or disappointments at some level in your life? Most people have. Come with me to a place called Beyond—beyond our failures, beyond our self-doubts, beyond our disappointments, and beyond our fears. It is time to renew your faith to trust in God's unceasing love and endless mercy to take the next step in your walk with Him. Ray Petty explores Going Beyond:

- PRESS into God's best—His goodness and greatness.
- BELIEVE that God takes the worst & turns it to our best.
- EXPERIENCE more than we can ask, think, believe, or imagine.
- WATCH God work all things together for our good and His glory.

Let this book take you to a place called "Beyond" to experience the extravagance of God's love and His ability to do in us and through what we cannot do on our own. Thirteen lessons for individual or group study.

ISBN: 9781602731059 • 202 pages • 5.5x8.5 in • $12.95 USD

JOURNEY IN DISCIPLESHIP STUDY GUIDE

This powerful stand-alone study guide by Ray Petty, issues a call to become a relevant follower of Christ as an agent of change in your world. Through these 16 Bible lessons, you will gain a foundation for your service and a practical road-map into becoming more like Jesus Christ. This is for use in your individual or group study to find answers about:

- Revealing God's explosive power in YOUR life.
- Finding YOUR place in Christian community.
- Wielding God's Word for YOUR victorious living.
- Functioning in YOUR supernatural wholeness.

ISBN: 9781602730939 • 202 pages • 5.5x8.5 in • $10.95 USD